LAND BIRDS OF ALASKA
A FIELD GUIDE FOR CHILDREN

The <u>I Saw It!</u> Series #4: Field Guides, Journals, and Coloring Books for Children

by

Barbara L. Brovelli-Moon

Artwork by John C. Lofgreen

Junior Naturalist_____ **Date**_____

ANCHORAGE, ALASKA

Brovelli-Moon, Barbara L. (Illustrator, John C. Lofgreen)
Land Birds of Alaska: A Field Guide for Children
The I Saw It! Series #4: Field Guides, Journals, and Coloring Books for Children

ISBN: 978-0-9962559-5-0

Published by OceanOtter Publishing
Designed by Phillip Gessert
Edited by Norma Neill, Hannah Frenier, and Gregory Jefferies
Printed in the United States of America

10 9 8 7 6 5 4 3 2 1

Contact the author at oceanotterpublishing@gmail.com or www.oceanotterpublishing.com

Table of Contents
And Checklist of Sightings

Introduction i

Why Do We All Have Three Names? ii

Parts of a Bird iii

Grouse

❏ Spruce Grouse..2

❏ Willow Ptarmigan 4

Hawks, Eagles

❏ Northern Harrier 6

❏ Bald Eagle 8

❏ Golden Eagle 10

Cranes

❏ Sandhill Crane 12

Owls

❏ Great Horned Owl.....................................14

❏ Short-eared Owl 16

❏ Snowy Owl..18

Hummingbirds

❏ Rufous Hummingbird................................20

Kingfishers

❏ Belted Kingfisher.......................................22

Woodpeckers

❏ Downy Woodpecker...................................24

Falcons

❏ Gyrfalcon 26

❏ Peregrine Falcon.......................................28

Jays, Magpies, Crows

❏ Gray Jay 30

❏ Steller's Jay...32

❏ Black-billed Magpie 34

❏ Northwestern Crow 36

❏ Common Raven...38

Swallows

❏ Tree Swallow...40

Chickadees

❏ Black-capped Chickadee............................42

Nuthatches

❏ Red-breasted Nuthatch 44

Kinglets

❏ Ruby-crowned Kinglet...............................46

Thrushes

❏ American Robin 48

❏ Varied Thursh 50

Waxwings

❏ Bohemian Waxwing 52

Wood Warblers

❏ Wilson's Warbler.......................................54

❏ Yellow Warbler 56

Sparrows

❏ Fox Sparrow 58

❏ Savannah Sparrow.....................................60

❏ Dark-eyed Junco 62

Finches

❏ Pine Grosbeak 64

❏ Common Redpoll 66

❏ Pine Siskin..68

Common Bird Group Names 70

Beaks are Bills!..71

Glossary..72

Learn More About......................................74

Acknowledgements

Thanks, Mikey Kemmer, for the initial idea for these books. John Lofgreen, your art is amazing! The drawings are exactly what I wanted. Thank you for your attention to detail and willingness to do and redo. Also, the painting on the cover of this book is striking and brilliant. Thank you for letting me use it. Norma Neill, friend, editor, and cheerleader - I could not have done these books without you. Thanks for the expertise, ideas, long hours, giggles, and donuts. Hannah Frenier, editor and bird advisor, thank you! Your expertise in editing was so helpful. I especially thank you for sharing experiences and stories from your lifelong relationship with these feathered wonders. They became even more fascinating and alive. Sakura Likar, thanks for being ready to offer a new perspective. Brayden Battle of Battleboys' Graphics, your coloring is superb! Gene Dickason, thanks for always having the right photograph. Special thanks to Dr. Tuula Hollman of the Alaska Sea Life Center in Seward, Alaska, for helping with the list and information for this book. Also, thanks to Laurie, Jeff, and Darin, the education team at the Center. I'm so grateful for you seeing the value of this series in promoting empathy for and understanding of our amazing animal world. Hugs to all the Seagals in Brookings, Oregon. And Greg and Maggie, WE did it again! Let's keep on keeping on, laughing as we wander.

Cover painting by John C. Lofgreen

Back cover drawing colored by Brayden Battle

Introduction

Hello, and welcome to the world of birds. What is a bird, you ask? A bird is a warm-blooded vertebrate (an animal with a backbone) that lays eggs, has a beak, feathers, and wings, and is able to fly. The male of most bird species has brighter, more colorful feathers and plumage. This helps him attract females and claim his territory. The duller female coloring draws less attention, which protects her when she is nesting and caring for baby birds. Colorful or dull, birds are designed to fly. Their strong bones are hollow and very light. They flap their wings powerfully with the help of strong muscles in their breasts and wings. The shape of their wings, along with their feathers, allow them to push against the air and to soar freely above us all.

This book, *Land Birds of Alaska*, is . . .

. . . a field guide in which thirty-four land birds tell their own stories. You will learn where they live, what they eat, how they act, and so much more.

. . . a journal that gives you a place to write your own story about seeing these birds. Where were you? Who was with you? What happened? Keep a record of your experiences as you see these amazing feathered creatures.

. . . a coloring book for you to color the image of each bird. Follow the descriptions given to color them accurately, or color them pink, green, orange, or purple. This is your book to use as you choose.

The book also includes a checklist to record when you have seen one of the birds, an explanation of the differences between common and scientific names, a chart that gives the group name of a species, a glossary, and other hidden surprises!

Enjoy getting to know these amazing birds who live in Alaska!

Key to Range Maps

Year-Round Winter

Summer Fall/Spring

Why Do We All Have Three Names?

Hello from Alaska! I'm Oscar Snowy Owl, here to tell you why each bird in this book has three names at the top of its story page. On my page, you will see . . .

Snowy Owl
ukpik in Inupiat • *Bubo scandiacus*

The first name listed is my common or popular name, the one English-speaking people use when they talk about me. That name is **Snowy Owl**. The second name listed is the common name in one of the more than twenty Alaska Native languages. I am known as *ukpik* in the Inupiat language. A Native name is provided to introduce you to some of these beautiful, old languages. My name is not capitalized in this Native language, but sometimes our names are capitalized.

The last name listed is my scientific name, ***Bubo scandiacus***. Everything living on our planet has a scientific name created by scientists. These complicated names are used to be absolutely positive about the identity of the life form being discussed or studied. Seven classifications, or divisions, make up my long scientific name:

Kingdom, **Phylum**, **Class**, **Order**, **Family**, **Genus**, and **Species** ("**K**ids **P**refer **C**andy **O**ver **F**resh **G**reen **S**alad" will help you remember!)

Kingdom is the largest classification, and each division after that becomes more and more specific. My entire scientific name is below, with a brief explanation of the characteristics or meaning of each classification.

Classification	Name	Characteristics/meaning
Kingdom	Animalia	Animal
Phylum	Chordata	Vertebrate or an animal with a backbone
Class	Aves	Any bird
Order	Strigiformes	Owls, and other like birds
Family	Strigidae	Typical owl
Genus	*Bubo*	Horned owl
Species	*scandiacus*	Snowy owl

A scientific name is based on a Latin or Greek word. "Animalia" comes from the Latin "animale," and "aves" is the Latin word for "bird." Complete scientific names are so long scientists use only the last two categories, genus and species, when they talk about me or any other life form.

That is why my scientific name in this book gives you only my genus and species, ***Bubo scandiacus***. Now you know!

Parts of a Bird

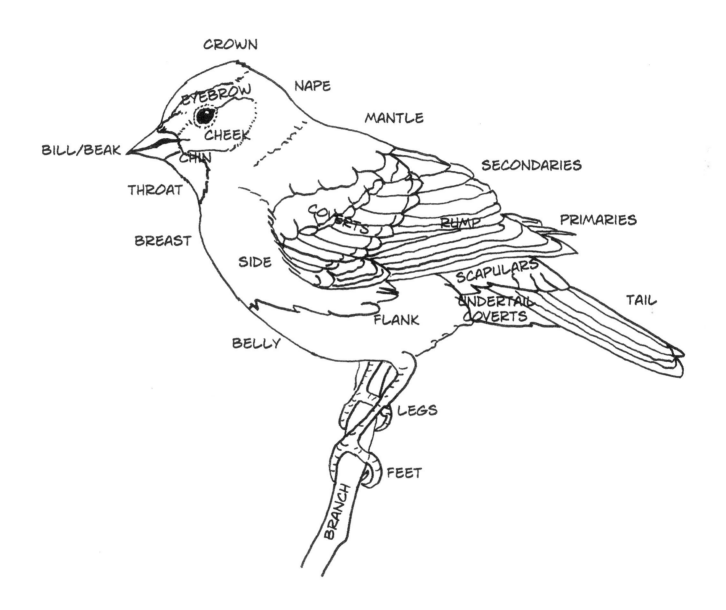

CROWN

NAPE

EYEBROW

MANTLE

CHEEK

SECONDARIES

BILL/BEAK

CHIN

THROAT

COVERTS

RUMP

PRIMARIES

BREAST

SIDE

SCAPULARS

UNDERTAIL
COVERTS

TAIL

FLANK

BELLY

LEGS

FEET

BRANCH

Spruce Grouse

káax' in Tlingit • Falcipennis canadensis

Um, hello! I'm GusGus Spruce Grouse, smallest of the four species of grouse in Alaska. I'm also called Fool's Hen and Spruce Hen or Chicken. I look like a medium-sized chicken, and as for the fool's part . . . well, some do say I am not as smart as other birds. Sometimes I sit absolutely still, even if someone walks right up to me. I might wander into a grouse hunter's campsite or pick strawberries with you in your garden. Does that mean I'm not smart? Maybe I'm just extremely tame, or curious, or . . . whatever.

You'll have to be smart to see me, though, whether I'm sitting in a conifer tree in the lush, boreal forest, or squatting in the mossy undergrowth of berry bushes and shrubs. I'm naturally camouflaged with black feathers covering my chest and neck, and dark, brownish-black feathers on the rest of my body. The ends of my dark feathers have white bars that look like spots of sunlight flickering through the trees. Hens are even harder to spot with their dark rusty- or grayish-brown feathers and thick, white bars. Both of us have short, dark tails with reddish-brown tips.

Watch in the spring when it is time for me to look for a mate. My bright, red combs stand straight up over my dark, beady eyes. Only we cocks, or males, have these combs, which are just one of the fancy ways I have to attract a hen. I also strut proudly, fan my tail, and point it upward instead of downward. Next, I stiffen my wings and beat them on the ground as fast and hard as I can. Finally, I puff out the feathers on my neck and chest to look even more handsome.

In the winter, though, I'm not so fancy. I spend much of my time cuddled in the snow roost I make to stay warm and hidden away from predators. I digest the tough conifer needles I've eaten during the day and stored in my crop, or special pouch in my neck. Then, while I roost, the needles move to my stomach, which has two parts. One part makes a strong liquid that begins dissolving the needles, and the other part, my gizzard, grinds up the softened needles. I swallow sharp, hard pieces of rock that stay in my gizzard to help chop up the needles. All this grinding gives me the food I need to stay strong and healthy.

So watch for healthy me . . . a hidden grouse in a spruce tree!

My Facts

SIZE: Length: 16 - 18 inches. Weight: 14 - 17 ounces. Wingspan: 20 - 23 inches.
COLOR: Male: Body: chest/neck, solid black; sides/underparts, black with white spots/bars. Female: Body: dark rusty- or grayish-brown; chest/underparts, same as body with thick, white bars. Both: Tail: short, dark, light-brown tip (Southeast birds have white spots on tip).
FOOD: Herbivorous. Summer/fall: flowers, green leaves, berries (especially blueberries and mountain cranberries). Winter: spruce needles.
VOICE: Male: guttural clicking noises, hoots, croaks, low hoots *whoop-whoop-whoop*. Female: same sounds, with some more high-pitched.
LIFESPAN: 3 - 10 years.

Did You See Me? Tell Your Story! _____

_____

_____

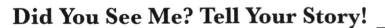

DID YOU KNOW? I seem tame, but if another cock enters my territory, I am mean and aggressive. Even hens fight among themselves at times! In the winter, I may roam a few miles from home and might even join a small flock. Usually, I'm alone and content.

Willow Ptarmigan

lacbe in Ahtna • Lagopus lagopus

Oh, my! It's springtime, and I'm molting again. Tina Turnagain Ptarmigan's (TARm-again) the name, and I'm turning a different color . . . again. My all-white winter coat helped me hide in the winter snow, but that snow is melting now. I need to blend in with the brownish ground colors that are beginning to show, so I'll be patchy brown and white for a while. Then, my rusty-brown feathers will be my coat through the summer and into the fall when I become patchy again. (My wings stay white *all* the time.) By winter, I'll turn back to my all-white coat. See why I'm called "Turnagain?"

Changing colors is the perfect way to camouflage myself. You see, I'm a very popular "game bird." I am the largest of the three ptarmigan species that live in Alaska, and hunters love my chunky body. Those dangerous hunters find me in more parts of the state than the others in my family, too. I live in moist thickets of willow shrubs in arctic valleys, on the marshy arctic and alpine tundra, along the coast, in muskeg or swampy areas, and in the mountain foothills. I hide in thick bushes almost everywhere!

Hiding and being well camouflaged don't help with our basic population problem, however. Only about one-fourth of our chicks survive their first year! When lots of chicks are born, it's not that serious, but when a low number of chicks hatch, it's terrible. For some unknown reason, we go through these "boom or bust" cycles every nine to ten years. Either plenty of us hatch and survive or just a few. It's very strange!

It's strange, too, how protective my mate is when I have our chicks. (I have a new mate each spring.) No other male in the grouse family is so involved. My mate finds a bowl-shaped space on the ground, protected by shrubs, for our nest. Together, we line it with leaves, grass, and feathers. After I lay four to ten brown-spotted, yellow eggs, my mate protects me while I hatch the clutch. Then, he helps me protect our chicks from large birds, raptors, and small mammals who love to eat our eggs and young!

With all this help, I will survive. I must, for I am the official state bird of Alaska. In 1955, Alaska was about to become the forty-ninth state. School children chose me to be the new state's bird. The mosquito is not the state bird, and I want you to see what your state bird looks like. I know you'll see lots of mosquitoes!!

My Facts

SIZE: Length: 15 - 17 inches. Weight: 19 - 20 ounces. Wingspan: 22 - 24 inches.
COLOR: Male: Spring/summer. Body: back/sides, rusty brown; belly/wings, white; tail, black. Head: bill, dark; above eyes, orange-red combs (darker when courting and breeding). Female: Spring/summer. Body: warm brown, yellowish barring speckled with black. Head/neck: reddish brown; belly/wings, white. Both: Winter. Body: white; tail, white with dark-edged tip. Both: Summer/all year. Body: wing flight feathers, white; legs/feet, white feathers. Head: eye-rings, white.
FOOD: Herbivorous. Summer: willow and other buds, green shoots, leaves, flowers, buds, seeds, berries. Winter: willow twigs, buds, some birch and alder.
VOICE: Male: deep clucks, croaks, noisy *go-back, go-back, kwow-kwow*. Female: noisy clucks, croaks, cackles, purrs, and moans with chicks.
LIFESPAN: 2 - 3 years.

Did You See Me? Tell Your Story!

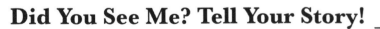

_____

_____

_____

DID YOU KNOW? In the fall, females and offspring flock together to spend the winter in southern parts of Alaska. (Males stay further north.) We feed and roost together until spring. Then, we return to our breeding areas to stay with a mate until the next fall.

Willow Ptarmigan 5

Northern Harrier

naptak in Yupik • Circus cyaneus

Harriette Harrier here, the only type of harrier in North America. What's a harrier, you ask? I'm a unique hawk, with a slender body, long, somewhat rounded wings, and a long, rounded tail. I once was called a "marsh or field hawk" because I love wide-open spaces! I live in freshwater and tidal marshes, open fields, out on wet or dry tundra, and throughout treeless grasslands. You can spot me flying very low to the ground, with shallow, smooth wingbeats, floating into a lazy glide. I tip from side to side, my wings held in an obvious "V" position. I do soar high in the sky like other hawks when I am migrating south, but that's not my usual place to be.

I'm different from other hawks in the way I hunt, too. They sit on high perches watching for prey, or chase helpless songbirds through the air. I fly close to the ground, listening as well as looking for my prey. Though I'm not an owl, I do have a stiff, feathered disc around my face just like some owls. These disc feathers direct sound waves to my ears to help me *hear* the quiet rustling of hidden prey when I'm flying low looking for food. Once I hear or see my victim, I hover (HUV-er) above it, just for a second, then make a quick pounce to grab it with my sharp talons. I land smoothly, holding my meal, and the ground becomes my dinner table.

If you do see me eating, or flying for that matter, you might be confused. My coloring, and the colors on our males, are more varied than those of any other bird of prey. My back and head are brown, and my underparts are light tan with brown streaks. Males have pale-gray backs and heads, and their underparts are whitish with brown spots. It looks like they have tipped the end of their wings in black paint, too. Our youngsters look like me except their chests are pumpkin orange. We all have obvious white rumps and bright, yellow legs. With our varied coloring, it looks like we are each a completely different species!

Speaking of young, I lay four to six white eggs each spring in my nest, hidden on the ground in a thick clump of sedges or reeds. In about a month, my eyas (EYE-es), or babies, hatch, and within two weeks they are walking near the nest. By the time they are a month old, they start to fly, close to the ground where all harriers fly. If you look carefully, I'm sure you will spot me.

My Facts

SIZE: Female larger. Length: 16 - 20 inches. Weight: 11 - 26 ounces. Wingspan: 40 - 46 inches.
COLOR: See story.
FOOD: Carnivorous. Summer: voles, shrews, mice, hares, songbirds, occasionally amphibians or fish. Winter: voles, shrews, mice.
VOICE: Varied shrill whistles *pee-pee-pee, kee-kee-kee, or sseew-sseew-sseew.*
LIFESPAN: 12 - 15 years.

Did You See Me? Tell Your Story! _____

_____

_____

DID YOU KNOW? I spend the winter in open fields and unfrozen marshes, away from freezing, snowy areas. Our population is declining due to people building where we live and pesticides killing our food supply. It's critical that I find food and open spaces!

Bald Eagle

kuckalaq in Alutiiq • Haliaeetus leucocephalus

Greetings. I am Bald Eagle, national symbol of these great United States. I have no "human name" as I represent *all* of you. I became our country's sign of strength and freedom long ago due to my fierce beauty and strong independence. You will see me on money, stamps, passports, and even the President's official seal.

I *am* unique and majestic! My large body is extremely impressive, with its rich, black feathers and magnificent large, white head. My rounded tail becomes white after four or five years. Notice my long, hooked, yellow beak, and my unusually large, shiny, yellow eyes which see three times as far as you see. I am a raptor, a bird of prey. That means I eat meat, using my strong feet and sharp talons to catch my prey.

On wings spreading almost eight feet across, I cruise about twenty-five miles per hour. I speed up to sixty miles per hour when I chase prey, and up to one hundred miles per hour if I dive after a victim. When flying, I straighten my wings and move them in slow, shallow wingbeats. During my fall migration, I save energy by "riding the thermals." Wings still, I soar skyward on the rising currents of warm air, then fall into long, smooth, downward glides.

Save *your* energy! Look for me only in North America, especially in Alaska. More than thirty thousand of us live here, about half our population. I'm usually near bodies of water . . . oceans, large lakes, rivers, marshes, and tidal flats hunting for my primary food, fish. I do fly into forests and woodlands if they are near water. I'm usually alone, but occasionally you'll see me with others. We feed on salmon as they run up the rivers and on waterbirds who have gathered.

I'm not alone from April to October, either, when I join my mate-for-life to have our eaglets, or young. My mate and I don't migrate nor spend the winter together, but each spring, we both return to our enormous eyrie (AIR-ee) built on the top of a tree. We enlarge the nest each year, and right now it is five feet across weighing over a thousand pounds! The large branches, with sticks, moss, leaves, and grasses holding them together, have become very heavy. Our nest must be strong to hold our young as they grow into the majestic birds that symbolize our amazing country.

My Facts

SIZE: Female larger. Length: 31 - 37 inches. Weight: 9 - 14 pounds. Wingspan: 6 - 8 feet.
COLOR: Body: dark brown/black; tail, white; legs, bright yellow. Head: white; bill, bright yellow. Immature: body/tail, brown with white spotting; underwing/bill, black.
FOOD: Carnivorous. Mainly fish, including salmon, herring, flounder, pollack; also small mammals, small birds, waterfowl, clams, crab, carrion, roadkill.
VOICE: Variety of calls: high-pitched whistles, cackles, squeaky chitters, thin squeals *kleet-kik-ik-ik-ik.*
LIFESPAN: 20 - 35 years.

Did You See Me? Tell Your Story!

_____

_____

_____

DID YOU KNOW? Long ago, we disappeared almost completely in the Lower 48 due to pesticides, illegal hunting, and land destruction. In 1940, laws were passed to protect us, and in 2007, we were taken off the Threatened and Endangered Species lists.

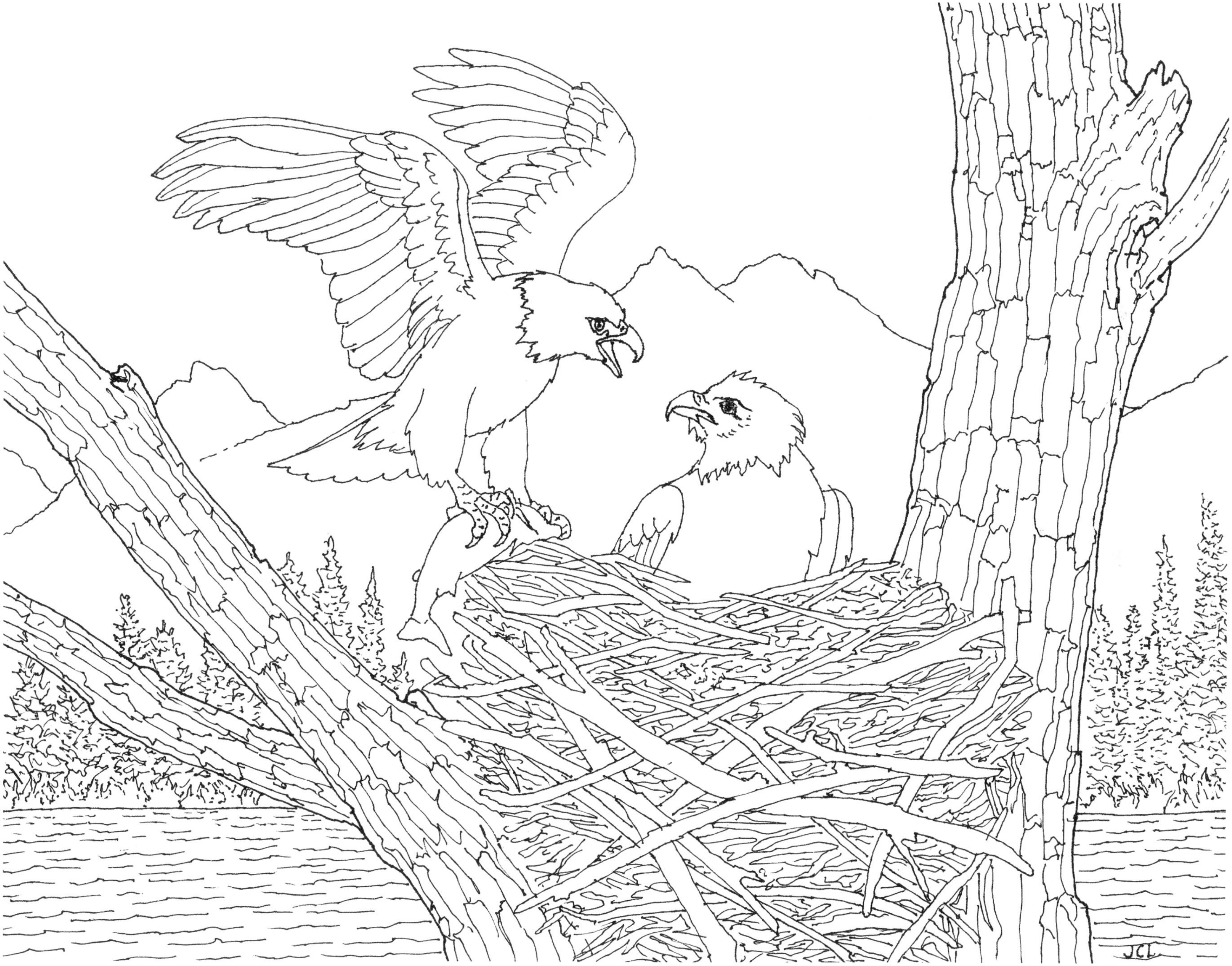
JCL

Golden Eagle

tilila in Koyukon • Aquila chrysaetos

I am Golden, the golden eagle, both feared and revered as the largest bird of prey in North America. High in the sky, soaring smoothly and majestically, I glide and "wheel" as I ride the wind. My long, rounded, powerful wings extend fully and lift slightly. I'm peaceful and graceful with my slow, smooth, shallow wingbeats.

Be aware, though. I am a raptor, a deadly predator. I'm always watching for movement on the ground far below. My eyes are like binoculars, and I see prey up to two miles away. Once my victim is in sight, I dive toward it at speeds up to two hundred miles per hour, never once losing track of my meal. With my strong legs, powerful feet, and razor-sharp, curved talons, I easily snatch and carry away a hare, marmot, or other small mammal. Then, using my terrifyingly strong, hooked beak, I tear the flesh from its bones to feast once again.

I am a dangerous, ruthless hunter, dropping from great heights or flying low over the ground to grab my prey. Other times, I sit quietly on a branch in a tree, waiting for my next meal to appear. I hunt in all types of terrain from the seashore to high in the mountains. I roam in upland, arctic tundra, through lowland shrubby areas, across grasslands, or along the edges of coniferous forests near streams and rivers. I fly over estuaries, mountain ridges, and open, wooded country. I don't go near people nor towns, so don't look there!

Watch in the fall as I migrate, wandering alone from Alaska to winter in warmer areas of the Lower 48. There, I soar over varied habitats hunting for small creatures until I return to Alaska in the early spring.

My mate-for-life, Glory, also returns from her winter migration, and we meet at our eyrie, or nest, built on the rocky ledge of a mountain cliff. (Some of us build nests in the tops of trees near riverbanks, too.) We repair our eyrie every year, adding sticks to the outside and fresh grasses, leaves, and mosses inside. Our nest has spread to six feet across and ten feet tall. Soon, Glory will lay one to four brown-speckled, white eggs. Sadly, only one or two of our hatched eaglets will survive to fledge at three months. Wolverines and grizzlies are just two enemies who kill our young

We *do* survive, though, so look skyward, and watch me soar!

My Facts

SIZE: Female much larger.
Length: 28 - 41 inches. Weight: 6.5 - 13 pounds.
Wingspan: 6 - 7.5 feet.
COLOR: Body: mainly dark chocolate-brown with lighter feathers on wings; tail, grayish brown with light bars; legs/feet, yellowish (with feathers). Head: nape/crown, golden, buff; eyes, dark brown; bill, dark grayish with black hook. Immature: brown with white spotting; underwings, white patches; bill, black.
FOOD: Carnivorous. Hares, marmots, squirrels, cranes, owls, ptarmigan, fish, carrion, large insects.
VOICE: Yelping bark *kya-kya* or *kee-kee-kee*. Seldom heard.
LIFESPAN: up to 32 years.

Did You See Me? Tell Your Story! _____

_____

_____

DID YOU KNOW? Our young look similar to juvenile bald eagles. Ours have smaller heads, and white patches under their wings and at the base of the tail. Also, all of us have feathers on our legs clear to our toes. Bald eagles are bald, even on their legs. Ha!

Sandhill Crane

dal. in Haida • Grus canadensis

Carolyn Crane, checking in! I'm here with my mate-for-life, Carl, and our colt, or youngster, Cara. Carl and I returned to this grassy marsh in early May, and we began dancing immediately. We are energetic, long-legged, wading birds who love to dance. When we were three or four years old, it was the way we attracted a mate. Now that we are together forever, we dance to keep our relationship strong. Watch as we stretch our long wings upward, pump our red-fronted heads, skip, bow, and leap into the air. Sometimes we toss grass or sticks to each other, and sometimes Cara joins us!

In addition to dancing when we returned, Carl and I gathered grasses and sedges to build our large, simple nest. I laid two, grayish-brown, spotted eggs in the middle of the cup-shaped, grass-lined hollow. After a month, with both of us taking turns sitting on the eggs, our colts hatched. They were fully developed, covered with soft down, with eyes wide open. They walked that same day. Carl and I brought food to them, and they were also catching insects on their own. Tragically, our son chased a deerfly too far from us, and before we could do anything, a bald eagle swooped down and carried him off! We hissed, leapt high in the air, flew at that eagle, and kicked our feet trying to save our son. It was no use. We've fought off foxes, coyotes, and owls, so at least we still have our three-week-old Cara.

Cara will be ready to join us this fall when we leave the muskeg, tundra, and bogs to fly south. We'll follow the Pacific Flyway to Central California for the winter. (Eastern family members go to other areas in the lower 48.) We'll travel with thousands of our kind in massive flocks, flying during the daytime in good weather. Our flocks fly in great, circling columns as we ride the warm, upward currents of air. Our "V" formations will be so high you probably won't see us. If you do, you'll notice that our legs are straight out behind us and our long necks stretch way out in front. (Other wading birds tuck their necks back when they fly.) We fly with slow, rolling, downward wingbeats, but quick, snapping upbeats. At night, we roost together on shallow lakes or rivers where it's safe. Be aware that we are extremely nervous around your kind. *Stay back*, or we will *hissssss* very loudly at you, then quickly fly away!

My Facts

SIZE: Male larger. Height: 3 - 4 feet. Weight: 7 - 10 pounds. Wingspan: 5 - 6 feet.
COLOR: Body: slate gray (reddish-brown staining from mud in bogs and muskeg); upper throat/cheek, whitish; legs, black. Head: chin/bill, black; crown/forehead, dull red. Immature: gray and rusty brown; no pale cheek nor red crown.
FOOD: Omnivorous. Summer: nearly anything on the ground or in shallow water, including amphibians, reptiles, plants, roots, berries, insects, invertebrates, small mammals. Winter: grains, wheat, insects, summer foods as available.
VOICE: Rattling, loud *kar-r-r-r-o-o-o.*
LIFESPAN: 12 - 20 years.

Did You See Me? Tell Your Story! _____

_____

_____

DID YOU KNOW? I have an unmistakable, powerful voice! My long windpipe loops in my chest, helping me create a loud, rolling, musical sound. Listen for a low-pitched, rich trumpet. That's me. I'm loudest during mating season, but I'm never quiet!

Great Horned Owl

umunyk in Yupik • Bubo virginianus

Who, who, who are *you*? *I am* Odysseus Owl, the great horned owl. Of all common owls in North America, I am the largest, most powerful, and most familiar. Do you recognize me from my picture in storybooks or my parts in movies? I am the "hoot owl," the symbol of wisdom, knowledge, and luck. I stand tall, with a short neck and long, feathered tufts that look like horns atop my rounded head. See the dark "V" dropping down my forehead to break the round disc of feathers on my face? Humans describe me as wise, strong, and stunning. I may be all that you say I am, but first and foremost, I am a bird of prey, a predator, who terrorizes many and fears few.

In fact, I have no natural predators. Rather, *I* am the fierce hunter, perched silently on a tree branch, watchful and endlessly patient. My large, yellow, catlike eyes are binoculars, allowing me to see the slightest movement far away, even at night. My victim spotted, I swoop down, gliding silently on steady wings with their long flight feathers. These feathers have soft, irregular edges, not like those of other birds with their straight, stiff edges. When air strikes my uneven feathers, no sound is made, no warning given. The small mammal or bird who has wandered into my territory never hears me as I snatch it with my death-grip talons, breaking its backbone with a grasp no one escapes. As my hooked beak tears its flesh, I enjoy, once again, a very tasty meal.

Silent wings and talons are not the only tools I have to capture my prey. My incredible eyes aim only forward, never moving from side-to-side. My entire head, however, swivels and turns. I see to the front, the side, and backward without moving my eyes! As my head turns, the feathers on my face and the feather tufts atop my head catch sound waves given off when something moves. My ears, hidden under the dark edges of my facial disk, pick up these sounds as far away as nine hundred feet. (That's ten times further away than you can hear!) As I listen, turn my head, then listen more, I find the exact location of the movement. Once again, a victim is found.

Know that *you* will be found if you come into the forest and onto my two square miles of territory. Be aware that I will watch you carefully while I ask, "Who, who, who are *you*?"

My Facts

SIZE: Female larger. Length: 21 - 25 inches. Weight: male, 3 pounds; female, 4 pounds. Wingspan: 4 - 5 feet.

COLOR: Body: grayish to white (white in arctic); belly, white with brown and black barring and mottling. Head: face, tawny orange to white; throat, white; eyes, yellow; ear tufts, darker than rest of head; bill, black.

FOOD: Omnivorous. Most diverse diet of all N. American raptors, includes snowshoe hares (favorite), other small and medium-sized mammals, birds, reptiles, fish, insects, invertebrates, carrion.

VOICE: Male: Series of five to eight loud, deep, muffled hoots, second and third shorter and faster; far-carrying *hoo-hoo-hoo, hu-hu-hu-hu, hoo-hoo;* also hisses, screams, bill-clapping. Female: Nasal barking *gu-waay;* higher pitched, shorter sequence. Immature. Screams; wheezy, or scratchy bark *reeek, sheeew.*

LIFESPAN: 12 - 20 years.

Did You See Me? Tell Your Story! _____

_____

_____

_____

DID YOU KNOW? I don't chew my food like most other birds. I swallow large chunks, and my stomach muscles grind up the soft parts. Bones, teeth, feathers, and fur are ground up in my gizzard, or second stomach. These become the pellets that I vomit up.

Short-eared Owl

k'a´kw • Asio flammeus

Oh, hi! I'm Olga Owl, a crow-sized owl with tiny ear tufts. My kind lives all over the world except in Australia and Antarctica. I'm uncommon, but be alert! You *might* see me. Know why? Unlike other owls, I hunt in the daytime, either early in the morning or when the sun is going down. In grassy, treeless areas, freshwater marshes and bogs, and on the lowland tundra, look carefully for me! Watch for my really unique, crazy way of flying. My long wings flap with deep beats that are totally jerky and irregular. I flop one way, then another, then all of a sudden, I stop and hover like a helicopter. I flutter without moving, staying in the same place in the sky. Crazy, eh?

Hovering is a terrific way to spot prey. With my super-strong eyesight and sensitive hearing, I quickly see and hear voles or other little critters trying to hide from me. Even when I fly straight ahead, low over open ground, I detect prey easily. Once I spot a critter, *whoosh!* I attack! I fly in close to the ground and snag my victim with my strong talons as I fly by. Then I land on the ground or a low, nearby perch to bite the back of my prey's skull with my strong beak. One bite brings instant death! I dine by swallowing my victim whole or tearing it into bite-sized chunks. Yum!

I hunt by myself, but I'm not always alone. In the winter, I go south where it is warmer and easier to find voles and other tasty rodents. (Voles are my very favorite, and I travel thousands of miles to dine on them.) During those colder months, I often roost on the ground with a few others. We rest or sleep in weeds and grass, hiding from the falcons, hawks, eagles, and larger owls who dine on *us.*

I'm not alone when I have my owlets, either. Each year, with a new mate, I lay five to seven creamy-white eggs in a grass-lined, rounded nest curved into the ground. It takes about three weeks for the owlets to hatch, and within a month, they fledge and are on their own. While they grow, my mate protects us, screaming or whining at enemies. He might even pretend to have a broken wing to make him look like easy prey. This draws an enemy's attention away from our nest!

So remember . . . If you pay attention during the day, you just might see me! Watch carefully!

My Facts

SIZE: Length: 13 - 17 inches. Weight: 9 - 17 ounces. Wingspan: 35 - 42 inches.

COLOR: Female darker. Body: pale tannish; breast/belly, vertical streaks of darker brown; upper wings (in flight), pale with buff patches and black marks at wrist and tip. Head: pale tannish; facial disk, see "Did You Know?"

FOOD: Carnivorous. Voles, mice, shrews, hares, muskrats, bats.

VOICE: Male: muffled, rapid series *poo-poo-poo.* Both: high, raspy barking; low, sneezy *kee-you, wow, waow, yow.*

LIFESPAN: 4 years.

Did You See Me? Tell Your Story! _____

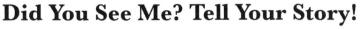

DID YOU KNOW? My ear tufts are very small and hard to see, but my facial disc is obvious. The light-tan feathers on the inside are outlined with a row of white feathers then a row of dark ones. My yellow eyes, outlined in black, look amazingly huge! I see you!

Snowy Owl

ukpik in Inupiat • Bubo scandiacus

Good day. I'm Oscar Snowy Owl, also known as the Arctic Owl, Great White Owl, Ghost Owl, Tundra Ghost, and White Terror of the North. I am a distinctive bird known far and wide. In fact, Hedwig, Harry Potter's owl, is a female version of myself. I live further north than any other owl, and I'm the heaviest of all the North American owls. Life's not all glamorous, though, for I have a serious problem.

I'm *horribly* dependent on lemmings for my survival. I *crave* those small rodents, swallowing them whole whenever possible! Oh, I'll eat voles, and I tolerate other creatures, like hares or even birds. Without my lemmings, though, I am *not* happy. Even the number of chicks our hens raise depends on the supply of lemmings available that year. Fewer lemmings means fewer eggs laid, so fewer chicks are born. In fact, during the winters with small lemming populations, hundreds of us leave the tundra of northern Alaska. We migrate south into the Lower 48 to find our favorite food. There's no warning about the lemming supply, either. They are here, or they are not. It's a very serious problem!

During normal years, when I don't have to migrate, I spend the winter in southern Alaska along lake or ocean shorelines, near marshes, or out in open fields. You might see me perched on the ground or on low posts around airports where there are open areas to spot my lemmings. (Have I told you I *love* lemming meat?) Then, in the spring, I return to my home in the treeless, arctic tundra where I find a new mate to share the responsibility of raising a clutch of chicks.

My mate and I raise the chicks together. She sits on our nest of white eggs until our white, downy chicks hatch. The chicks won't begin hunting on their own for about six weeks, so it's my duty to provide food for everyone until then. Usually I hunt during the daytime, but I will go out at night, too. I fly with strong, steady wingbeats, staying close to the ground. When I spot my prey, I sink my talons into it, break its neck with my beak, then take the whole creature back to my mate. She tears the food into chunks to feed our young.

Now, I must warn you. . . I tear chunks out of *any* predator who comes too close to our young, be it fox, jaeger, or even *you*. You've been warned, so I hope you stay far away!

My Facts

SIZE: Female larger. Length: 22 - 27 inches. Weight: 2.5 - 4.5 pounds. Wingspan: 4.5 - 5.3 inches.
COLOR: Male: Body: white with sparse, narrow, brown barring and spotting (more white with age). Female: Body: mainly white with more dark-brown barring and spotting. Both: Body: legs/toes, white (thickly furred). Head: eyes, yellow (small for owl); bill, dark. Immature: white with heavy, brown barring and spotting; face, all white.
FOOD: Carnivorous. Lemmings (mainly), voles, mice, hares, muskrats, marmots, ptarmigan, ducks, geese, fish, carrion.
VOICE: Male: Mainly silent with some loud, harsh, grating barks; when breeding *rick-rick-rick*, *kre-kre-kre*, *hoo-hoot*. Female: When breeding, higher-pitched *gruff-guy-huh-guk*.
LIFESPAN: 9.5+ years.

Did You See Me? Tell Your Story! _____

_____

_____

_____

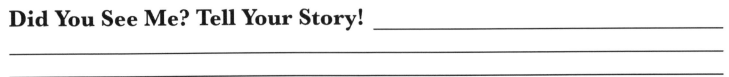

DID YOU KNOW? You might find my roosting branch by looking under trees for the pellets I've thrown up. When you open these, you will discover what I have been eating. I don't digest the bones, fur, or feathers of my victims, so these will be in my pellets.

JCL

Rufous Hummingbird

dagdagdiya'a in Haida • *Selasphorous rufus*

It's *me*! Hannah Rufous (ROO-fus) Hummingbird. I'm the smallest bird found in Alaska, measuring less than *four* inches long and weighing little more than a *penny*. Be warned, though. . . *YOU* are *not* the boss of me! I'm the *feistiest* of all hummingbirds, ready to attack you or *any* bird even *twice* my size who comes near *my* flowers or feeder. I dive-bomb, dart, and zip around, beating my wings more than one *hundred* flaps every *second*. (My wings make a humming sound you might hear before you see me.) I even fly *backward*, the only bird who does *that*. Avoiding me is *tricky*, but no one steals *my* food!

Most of my food is nectar, the sweet, sugary liquid found in flowers, especially *red*, tube-shaped ones. When I eat, I hover, or fly in one spot, *right* in front of my chosen flower. I extend my long, almost-straight bill into its center, and *Zip!* My long, forked tongue *darts* out to lick the nectar out of that flower. Some of your kind hang special, red-colored feeders filled with uncolored sugar water for *me* to drink. That's *delicious*! Sometimes I catch *insects* in midair, plucking them from leaves and twigs, or snagging them from a spider's web. I *much* prefer flowers or feeders, though!

I *was* the only hummingbird in Alaska until my cousin Anna Hummingbird was spotted in Southeast a few years ago! *I* go to Southeast every summer and fall, and even north into Anchorage. With *so* many hours of daylight during the summer, the flowers are *enormous* and *loaded* with nectar! I *always* return to my favorite gardens and flowers, too. *No!* I *don't* forget where they are, and Cousin Anna *better* stay away from *my* food! When the cold comes, though, the flowers die, so I fly south to find *blooming* flowers! I travel at least three *thousand* miles, the longest migration of *any* hummingbird in the United States! I go down through the Rocky Mountains, finding nectar-rich flowers in mountain meadows as high as twelve *thousand* feet. I end my trip at my *favorite* gardens in Mexico. Others in my family go to *their* flowers patches as far away as Panama or Florida.

Be alert! Look for me and *listen* for the humming of my wings along the edges of forests, in mountain meadows, and in parks and gardens where there are *bright* flowers. I fly straight at *any* flower I see, even fake flowers on your floppy hat, especially if they're *red*!

My Facts

SIZE: Length: 3.5 - 4 inches. Weight: 0.10 - 0.12 ounces (about 1.5 pennies). Wingspan: 4.3 - 4.5 inches.
COLOR: (Named for rufous, or reddish-brown, color.) Male: Body: back/belly, bright red-brown-orange; throat, iridescent red-orange. Female: Body: upper, shiny green; flanks, rufous; throat, white collar with orange. Both: Body: tail, white tipped with rufous throughout.
FOOD: Omnivorous. Nectar, tiny insects.
VOICE: (Wings make buzzy whistle or trill.) Call: high, hard, chippy *tyuk*; flight call, sputtering *zeee-chippity-chippity*. Male: low hum.
LIFESPAN: 3 - 10 years.

Did You See Me? Tell Your Story! _____

_____

_____

DID YOU KNOW? My small, compact, cup-shaped nest is made of grasses, moss, and other soft materials. Built high in a tree, it holds my two, white eggs, the smallest of any bird's eggs. Alone, I raise and feed my chicks until they fledge at about two months.

Belted Kingfisher

tlaxaneis' in Tlingit • Megaceryle alcyon

I'm Kira Belted Kingfisher, and *no!* I'm *not* having a bad hair day. That's just my unique crest of feathers that grows on the top and down the back of my large, shapely head. Every kingfisher has this shaggy, bushy crest all year long, so it's a good way to recognize me. The hairdo on the big head on a stocky, medium-sized body means kingfisher. Plus, I have short legs with unique, syndactyl (sin-DAC-till) feet. That means my middle toes are partly joined together. Why? Nobody knows.

Everyone does know that I have a long, straight, thick, dagger-like bill, though. This bill is my fishing rod that I use to catch my favorite food . . . fish. Watch for me either perched on a branch over a stream, river, pond, or other non-frozen water, or hovering above the water like a helicopter, my wings beating rapidly. (Just so you know, I usually fly very quickly, darting around with deep, irregular wingbeats.) I watch the water very carefully for small fish swimming near the surface. When I see my meal, I close my eyes and dive, zooming headfirst toward my prey. I smack the water without my body going under, and I pinch that fish in the tip of my bill. I immediately fly my prize back to my perch, and *whack*! I knock it on the branch to stun it. A stunned fish doesn't move, so I swallow the whole thing, head first, in one big gulp. Delicious!

By eating the entire fish without chewing, though, I have to deal with bones, fins, and the other parts I can't digest. Luckily, like owls, I have a gizzard, a special, muscular chamber at the beginning of my digestive track. My gizzard grinds up these hard, tough parts, then uses a thick, sticky liquid to glue them together into pellets. I cough up these pellets, then spit them out. Maybe you'll find one under my perch!

Look, too, for my nest chamber. Each year, a new mate and I dig a three- to six-foot long horizontal tunnel into a soft riverbank. Our nest, a burrow at the end of this tunnel, is where I lay five to eight smooth, glossy, pure-white eggs. These hatch in about twenty-two days, and after my mate and I feed the hatchlings for a month, they leave and are on their own. I'm on my own then, too, fishing and flying wherever I wander. Find me if you can!

My Facts

SIZE: Length: 11 - 13 inches. Weight: 5 - 5.9 ounces. Wingspan: 20 - 23 inches.
COLOR: Female more colorful (one of few). Body: dark blue-gray; belly/underparts, white with blue-gray breast band (female has additional rust-colored breast band); neck collar, white; wings/tail, fine, white spotting. Head: same as body; bill, black with white near face; spot in front of eye, white. Immature: same except irregular rusty spotting on breast band.
FOOD: Omnivorous. Fish, crayfish, other crustaceans, mollusks, amphibians, small reptiles, insects, small birds, berries.
VOICE: Loud, dry, long, uneven, clattering rattle when perched and in flight.
LIFESPAN: 5 - 7 years.

Did You See Me? Tell Your Story! _____

_____

_____

DID YOU KNOW? I'm the only kingfisher in Alaska and the most common one in North America. What's really special is our females are more colorful than our males! In most bird species, the males are more colorful. Can you figure out how our colors differ?

Downy Woodpecker

tuuyuk in Inupiat • Picoides pubescens

Tap! Tap! Tap! I'm Woodley Downy Woodpecker, the smallest woodpecker in North America. I'm about the size of a sparrow or chickadee, but size has nothing to do with noise level. I'm a wild and crazy drummer, rapping repeatedly on trees, branches, or other surfaces, with my sharp, chiseled, pointed bill. I whack a surface sixteen or seventeen times a *second*, pause, then drum again and again just like a jackhammer.

Annoying? Maybe, but drumming is important. I'm telling other woodpeckers to stay out of my five to thirty acres of forest. This is *my* territory year round, and if another of my kind invades, it's serious! I flick my wings, fan my tail, raise my chest and hold it high, signaling my invader to leave . . . *NOW!* If that bird doesn't, I attack by flying high into the air, then falling toward it, only to swoop high again and come in close enough to wrestle in midair. I fight, fight, fight to defend my territory!

If, however, the invader is a bird of prey, like a hawk or a falcon, or a larger woodpecker, it's a very different story. I hide behind a tree trunk or branch, clinging to the bark, as I wind slowly around the tree, staying out of sight. Sometimes I smash myself against the tree and stay completely still. I hold on for dear life by using my specially-designed feet and tail. My feet are zygodactyl (zy-go-DACK-til), meaning they have two toes in front and two in back, with strong, sharp claws on all four toes. I stick like glue. My tail has long, stiff feathers that help prop me up while I cling to the tree, too. I don't move a feather until the predator is gone.

Once I know I'm safe, I drum and tap again. I do slower, more irregular tapping to find food. I tap, tap, tap on a tree, then listen for insects or bugs to move under the bark. Then, I dig deeply into holes with my long, strong bill, and I use the bristles on the tip of my long tongue to grab my food. Other times, I probe into deep crevices or cracks in trees to find my meal. Our hens have shorter bills, so they pry insects from under the bark instead of digging into the wood. We *all* snatch yummy bugs off shrubs and large leaves throughout the forest, though.

Visit the forest soon, and listen. I'm sure you will hear me as I *tap tap tap*!!

My Facts

SIZE: Length: 6.0 - 6.75 inches. Weight: 0.75 - 1.0 ounces (same as a slice of bread). Wingspan: 9 - 12 inches.
COLOR: Body: upperparts, black with white stripe down back; underparts, white; tail, black with white; outer tail feathers, lightly spotted with black. Head: black with white stripes; bill, black with whitish tuft at base; eyes, black; male only, red patch on nape of neck.
Immature male: forehead, small red patch.
FOOD: Omnivorous. Insects, including flying insects, ants, beetles, weevils, caterpillars; also, spiders, berries, acorns, seeds.
VOICE: Flat *pik*; rapid, whinny notes going down in pitch; other chirps, squeaks, screeches.
LIFESPAN: 8 - 10 years.

Did You See Me? Tell Your Story! _____

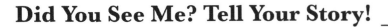

_____

_____

DID YOU KNOW? Woodward Hairy Woodpecker is almost my twin. He is larger than I am, has a longer, larger bill, and his outer tail feathers are completely white. We both have a broad, white stripe on our backs . . . the only woodpeckers with this stripe! Cool!

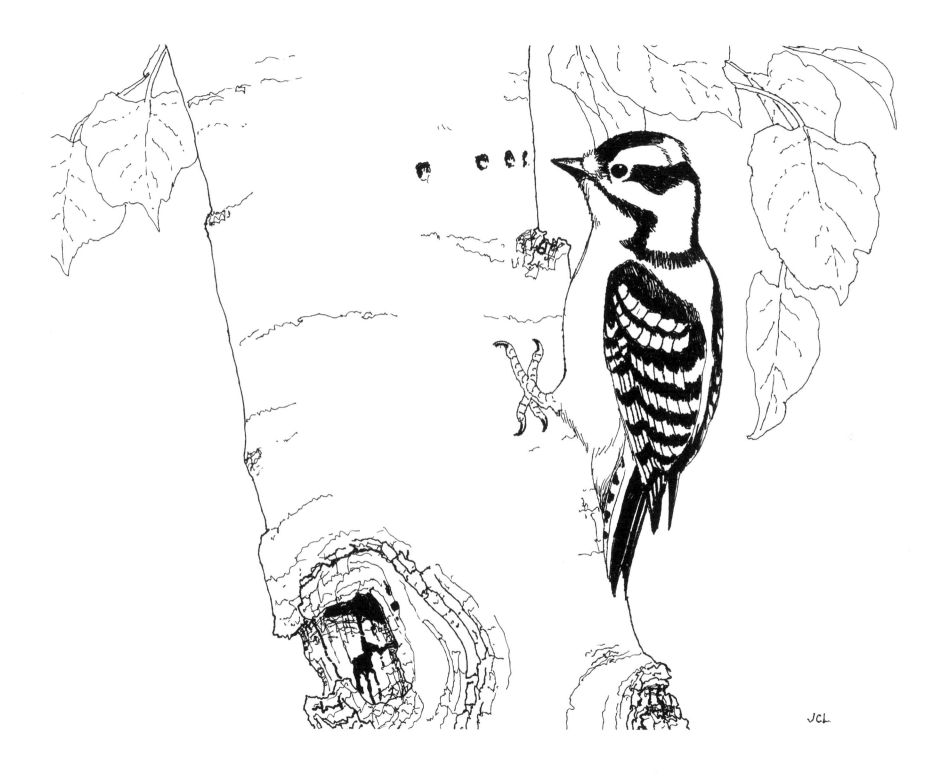

Downy Woodpecker 25

Gyrfalcon

kirgavik in Inupiat • Falco rusticolus

Good afternoon. I'm Glenda Gyrfalcon (JEER-falcon), the largest falcon in the world. Don't confuse me with my close cousin Fletcher Peregrine Falcon. I'm much larger and stockier than he is, have no dark helmet nor black patches on my head, and have wings that are wider at the base. Also, when I'm perched, my wings fold and cross much higher on my long, narrow tail.

My wings are amazing, beating slowly and so strongly when I fly. I move at breathtaking speeds as fast as fifty miles per hour, and I do incredible aerial dives from high in the air. Usually, though, I speed along closer to the ground, always watching for prey. Sometimes I fly in straight, level pursuit of my victim, chasing ptarmigan and small mammals through open tundra. I hunt for waterfowl along beaches and for smaller birds beside cliffs. I don't hunt in forests, as I need open spaces to overtake my victim. In fact, I love a long-distance chase, exhausting my prey, then forcing it down with one powerful blow from my strong talons. This breaks its back and breast bones. If I spot a victim hiding under a bush or shrub, I hover above it. This frightens the poor creature out into the open. Then I stoop, diving straight down to deal my death blow. Occasionally, I fly up and under my prey to strike a deadly blow to its underside. Once it falls to the ground, I feast alone, devouring the meat at my own pace.

I am alone except when I join my mate-for-life, Glenn, at our nest site in the early spring. For several years now, we have used a nest abandoned by Golden Eagle. The nest is on the ledge of a coastline cliff along the remote, northern arctic tundra. We find our favorite foods there, so I am able to cache a tasty hare, duck, ptarmigan, or other meal close to our nest.

It's fall now, though, so our young are raised and gone. I am on my own again, watching for prey from this rocky overlook. This is a good time for *you* to watch for *me*, as I will soon leave this faraway breeding area and move south to open coastal beaches and marshes. I find more food there during the winter, so look for me in open areas near unfrozen water. I'll be hunting for year-round ducks or geese. I might even be in towns hunting for small prey. Be patient, and very watchful!

My Facts

SIZE: Female larger. Length: 20 - 25 inches. Weight: 16 - 56 ounces. Wingspan: 48 - 60 inches.
COLOR: Body: color morphs from pure white to black, with gray most common; variable barring and spotting all over; legs, yellow. Head: eye-rings, yellow; eyes, black. Immature: similar to adult with more streaking on breast/belly; feet, blue gray.
FOOD: Carnivorous. Large birds, including ptarmigan, small hawks, owls, gulls, ducks, geese; small mammals, including voles, ground squirrels, hares.
VOICE: Deep, hoarse *kuah-kuah-kuah;* when alarmed, harsh, nasally *cack-cack-cack.*
LIFESPAN: 12 - 15 years.

Did You See Me? Tell Your Story! _____

_____

_____

DID YOU KNOW? For over four thousand years, I've been a favorite in the ancient sport of falconry. I was called the "bird of kings," as royalty wanted me for their games. Poachers still try to trap me, but I am protected now. It's illegal for anyone to capture me.

Peregrine Falcon

jaja ad. in Haida • Falco peregrinus

Good day. I'm Fletcher Falcon, one of the most common raptors found on all continents except Antarctica. What's not common about me is the black coloring covering the top of my head, extending down into distinctive, rounded wedges beneath my eyes. It looks like I'm wearing a helmet, and I *need* head protection. I fly faster than any other bird on the entire planet, stooping, or dive-bombing more than two hundred miles per hour when I target a duck, songbird, or other prey.

I'm a dangerous, ruthless hunter, soaring high in the sky. I watch for victims as far away as six miles. Once I spot my meal, I stop my powerful wingbeats, fold my pointed wings tightly against my body, aim my beak downward, and fall into a steep nosedive that hurls me earthward. I swoop down on my prey, and silently, without warning, attack in midair. Often, I close my taloned feet and punch my prey, sending it hurling to its death. Other times, I grab my victim, holding it with my sharp, pointed talons as I fly gently back to earth. Sometimes I hunt close to the ground, chasing my food at the speed of a running cheetah. No matter how I hunt, I feast after I've returned to land, eating slowly, savoring *every* bite.

I rely on my speed, also, when I'm wandering. My Latin name, *peregrinus*, means "wanderer," and that describes me perfectly! I migrate incredible distances, traveling as much as twenty thousand miles every year. In the fall, I move from the Arctic tundra to a distant South American desert, then return to Alaska in the spring. (My kind living in warmer areas don't travel as far, if at all.) Once I'm back in Alaska, I meet my same breeding mate at our eyrie (AIR-ee), or nest, where we raise three to five eyasses (EYE-a-sis), or chicks. Our young do well now, but raising chicks wasn't always possible.

You see, in the mid-20th century, farmers sprayed their crops with pesticides, like DDT, to kill insects. Small birds ate these dead insects and passed the poison on to us when we ate those birds. The poisons caused the shells of our eggs to be so thin they would break before hatching. The chicks all died, and we became endangered. Finally, poisons were banned and special groups raised us in captivity, then released us into the wild. In 1999, we were removed from the Endangered Species List. We are powerful, strong, and healthy again!

My Facts

SIZE: Female considerably larger. Length: 15 - 22 inches. Weight: 1 - 3.5 pounds. Wingspan: 36 - 41 inches.
COLOR: Body: upperparts, slate gray; wings, blue gray; underparts, buff white with dark barring on belly. Head: black; face, white with black tear stripe on cheek. Immature: upperparts, dark brown; underparts, light with heavy, dark streaking.
FOOD: Carnivorous. Birds, including ducks, shorebirds, pigeons, songbirds; small mammals, especially bats.
VOICE: Series of harsh *rehk-rehk-rehk;* at nest *kack-kack-kack-kack;* generally silent.
LIFESPAN: 17 years.

Did You See Me? Tell Your Story! _____

_____

_____

DID YOU KNOW? Throughout history, I have been valued by royalty for the sport of falconry. Even today, I am caught and trained by your kind to fly away, hunt for a bird, then return with it. But even as your captive, my spirit is wandering and free!

Gray Jay

stakalbaey<baa' in Ahtna • Perisoreus canadensis

Ah, ha! I'm Janey Jay with a question! How am I like Sophie Red Tree Squirrel? (Read about her in <u>Land Mammals of Alaska</u>.) Well, like Sophie, I *hoard* food! In fact, my Latin name, *"Perisoreus,"* means "hoarder." I collect and save food all summer long, caching it for the cold winter ahead. I don't migrate from this northern, boreal forest, so to survive the freezing winter, I store food. I collect everything from little water creatures to berries to bird eggs. I grab flying insects or bugs on trees and leaves, steal chunks of meat from dead animals in traplines, claim nuts or jerky left in an isolated cabin, and even rob food from your campsite. My nickname is "Camp Robber," the masked bandit, so don't be surprised if I fly right up and snatch a tasty peanut from your hand or a shiny key or spoon from your camp table. I'm a brave, insistent nuisance who's not afraid of you!

Sophie Squirrel stores her food in middens, or storage areas on the ground in her territory. I store my food differently. You know how you get spit in your mouth? Well, I do, too. In my mouth, I have large salivary glands that produce a whole bunch of sticky saliva, or spit. I wrap this sticky spit around each morsel of food I collect, then stick the gooey food behind flakes of bark on trees, in needles collected in the forks of trees, or under lichen growing on trees. All my food is stored high enough off the ground that the winter snow won't reach it, and pesky ground scavengers won't find it. On a busy day, I make over a thousand sticky caches, or storage sites. I remember where each one is, too!

I need all this food for myself, but my mate-for-life, Jake, and I both share our food with the chicks we raise during the coldest part of the winter. High in a thick conifer tree, we build our nest out of twigs and bark strips, then we line it with fur and feathers for warmth. In February or March, I lay three to five smooth, pale, gray-green eggs that are speckled with dark spots. The chicks hatch within three weeks. We take care of our nestlings until June, when the strongest chick chases the others away. Only that strong one stays in territory near ours for the rest of his or her life.

For the rest of *your* life, you'd better hide your camp food. I just might be *your* camp robber!

My Facts

SIZE: Length: 11.0 - 11.5 inches. Weight: 2.2 - 2.5 ounces. Wingspan: 16 - 18 inches.

COLOR: Body: back/legs, dark gray; underparts, light gray; tail, dark gray with pale tips. Head: nape/top of head, black to lighter gray; forehead/collar around throat, white; bill, black. Immature: sooty gray all over.

FOOD: Omnivorous. Arthropods, invertebrates, insects, small mammals, bird eggs, berries, human food.

VOICE: Varied shrill, high-pitched hoots, whistles, chatters, screams; low, husky *chuf-chuf-weef;* soft *whee-oh.*

LIFESPAN: 15 -17 years.

Did You See Me? Tell Your Story!

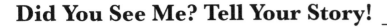

_____

_____

_____

DID YOU KNOW? Larger than Rosie Robin, but smaller than Jackson Steller's Jay, my stocky body has unusually thick, fluffy plumage. I puff up when the weather is cold, so my feathers cover even my legs, feet, and nose! Trapped air is warmed, which warms me!

Steller's Jay

x̱éishx'w. in Tlingit • Cyanocitta sterlleri

Hey! Want to know what's going on? Listen up, and I'll keep you posted on *all* the news. I'm Jackson Jay, one of the most intelligent, vocal songbirds in the mountain forests. I'm constantly talking in my noisy, harsh, scolding voice, except when it's breeding and nesting time. I whistle, rattle, and gurgle, plus I mimic the sounds of hawks, other birds, squirrels, and even your pet dog if I hear it. You'll hear me if you are anywhere in the mountain forests or by coastal, woodland areas. Listen anytime you're in campgrounds and parks, and even in your own backyard if you have tall trees. Just *listen*!

The first thing you need to hear is that I'm *NOT* a blue jay. Oh, we are both blue (I have black feathers, too, and he doesn't!), but that blue jay bird lives east of the Rocky Mountains. I live from those great mountains west to the Pacific Ocean. My name is much fancier, too. I'm named after naturalist George Steller, who saw me on an Alaska island when he traveled here with a Russian explorer in 1741. It was decided that he was the first to see me, so they gave me his name. (I was here long before he visited!)

Now, once you hear me, look for my beautiful, dark body. I'm sooty black in front and dark blue in back. Notice the long, shaggy, triangular crest on top of my head. I'm enormously proud of this headgear as I am the *only* western jay who has a crest. In addition, look for the very important, slight hook on my long, straight, thick bill. This hook helps me tear meat from little rodents I find when I hop along the ground, foraging, or looking for food. I flip my head from side to side, watching for the slightest movement. That rodent is mine if it moves at all, and I'll tear it apart!

Speaking of movement, my friends and I move around in small groups. We form flocks, except during breeding time, and hang out together. We play and chase each other, and we become quite aggressive when we group up to chase a hawk, owl, or other predators out of our space. We don't migrate, but we do move around in our local area if we need to find more food, or if the weather becomes a problem. We are fun-loving, noisy, obnoxious characters, ready at any moment to let you know what we think! So listen, will ya? I have plenty to tell you!

My Facts

SIZE: Length: 11.5 - 13.5 inches. Weight: 3.5 - 5 ounces. Wingspan: 17 - 19 inches.

COLOR: Body: front, sooty black; rear, deep to bright blue; legs, grayish blue. Head/crest: sooty black; forehead, sooty black with dark-blue streaks; eyes/bill, black. Immature: similar to adult; upperparts, washed with brownish gray; underparts, duller.

FOOD: Omnivorous. Seeds, nuts, berries, fruits, bird eggs, nestlings, invertebrates, small rodents, carrion.

VOICE: Varied harsh, scolding sounds; rattles; gurgles; snaps; pops; unmusical, descending *shaaaauur;* rapid *shack-shack-shack-shack-shack.*

LIFESPAN: 16 years.

Did You See Me? Tell Your Story!

_____

_____

_____

DID YOU KNOW? I am smart and unusually tame. If you hold peanuts, I'll land on your hand, pick up a small one, and throw it down my throat. Then I'll hold another in my mouth with a third one in my beak. I'll store these, then come back for more.

Black-billed Magpie

qalqerayak in Yupik • Pica hudsonia

Hi ya'll! I'm Marjorie Mae Magpie, put on this earth to be noisy and gregarious all day long. I fit in well with my family of jays and crows. I am one of only two magpies found in North America, and I feel it is my duty to let my voice be heard. My close cousin, Mallory Mei Magpie, with her yellow bill, lives only in California's Central Valley and nearby foothills. It is my responsibility to let the rest of the west know magpies exist!

Years ago, people said we were overdoing our need to be heard. They said, "You're pesky!" Many of my ancestors were actually killed for speaking out! Finally, laws were put in place to protect us and other birds. Now, I talk all I want, except . . . after funerals. Alas, when one of my kind is found dead, a shrieking call goes out. Being social and curious birds, as many as forty of us gather immediately to say goodbye to our departed kin. For ten or fifteen minutes, we all chatter, making a horrible racket. Then, abruptly, we stop. In silence, we fly away, returning to our prior tasks.

In the spring, I am also quiet during my job of nest building then raising my chicks. See the enormous nest my mate-for-life, Marshall, and I built? It's about thirty inches high and twenty inches wide. Along a stream, high in a tree with heavy branches, we spent about forty days putting together this structure. Marshall gathered sticks for the outside, while I built the interior using mud to form a cup. I lined it with weeds, grass, bark strips, and feathers. We made entrance holes on both sides of our basket-like nest. In late spring, I laid five, darkly-speckled, greenish eggs in the cup. After about twenty days, the chicks begin to hatch, one each day. Three are here, but sadly the other two didn't survive. Within thirty days, these three will begin flying, and by the time they are about two months old, they will fly away.

When the chicks leave, they look just like us. They'll have striking black-and-white plumage, shiny, iridescent green on their wings and tail, and white wing patches visible when they fly. They won't have our unusually long tail, however, until they are fully grown. They'll do our little hop before taking off to fly, and strut when they walk. So when you're out walking, look and listen for a black-and-white, chatty bird. That's me!

My Facts

SIZE: Length: 17.5 - 22 inches. Weight: 5.5 - 7 ounces. Wingspan: 22 - 24 inches.
COLOR: Body: upper breast/back/wings/tail, black with colorful iridescent-green patches; lower breast/belly/shoulder stripes by wings, white; legs, black; in flight, large patches of white on wings. Head/bill/eyes: black. Immature: same as adults; tail, shorter.
FOOD: Omnivorous. Insects, beetles, larva, eggs and hatchlings of songbirds, squirrels, voles, carrion, fruit, grains.
VOICE: Whining, rapid, high-pitched *mag-mag-mag* or *yak-yak-yak;* variety of trills, cackles, whistles.
LIFESPAN: up to 9 years.

Did You See Me? Tell Your Story! _____

_____

_____

_____

DID YOU KNOW? I've followed your kind for hundreds of years! Long ago, my ancestors stole scraps of bison killed by Plains Indians. My relatives even stole food from tents housing men on the Lewis and Clark expedition. I know you always have food for me!

Black-billed Magpie   35

Northwestern Crow

qanikcuk in Alutiiq • Corvus caurinus

Charlie Crow here, proud to tell you I'm the real deal . . . a true, omnivorous scavenger and habitual plunderer, with incredibly gross eating habits. I pig out on almost any "food" I find along the shoreline. Look for me from Kodiak Island, down through Southeast Alaska and the Canadian coast, to Puget Sound in the state of Washington. I scavenge in tidewaters, check out coastal bays and towns, look for seabird colonies, and thoroughly raid tide pools. I search river deltas, open woodlands, and along forest edges within seventy-five miles of the shore. The Pacific coast is *my* playground.

What am I looking for? You name it! Some of my favorites are blue bay mussels, clams, crab, sand dollars, and sea urchins. Any crustacean or small invertebrate is on *my* menu. I walk along the shore, dig in the sand, and wade in shallow tide pools looking for anything to scarf down. When I find a hard-shelled creature, I grab it and hold on as I fly high in the air above a rocky area. Then I drop my prey and watch its shell shatter on the rocks below. I swoop down immediately to gobble up the gooey meat inside! The stinky remains of dead seals, whales, and other marine mammals washed up on shore are incredible treats, too.

I don't limit myself to shore food. Amphibians I dig out from under rocks and fallen trees add special flavors. Fruit, especially blackberries, seeds, grains, nuts, and bird eggs contribute fiber and variety. Oh, and roadkill and carrion?

Those dead rodents and animals along highways are so tasty and full of bacteria! Garbage in cans without lids, big, open trash bins, and my favorite, the dump, add more to my table. I scratch and root through it all, finding unlimited treasures. I even peck dead bugs off the front of your car! Yum!

I'm not a guy who eats alone, either. Sometimes I hang out with just a small family band of two to eight others, but from late summer through winter, hundreds of us, all ages, join up in large, rowdy communities. We roam, roost, play, and eat together, even posting sentries to guard food we briefly cache. We create deafening sounds, with different signals and calls for different reasons, like when we need to mob-up and chase off hawks, owls, and other predators. Do I really play? You bet! I fly high, drop a stick or rock, then rush down to catch it. Ya gotta see it all, so look for the crow community! We are chomping food somewhere!

My Facts

SIZE: Male slightly larger. Length: 16 - 17 inches. Weight: 12 - 15.5 ounces. Wingspan: 33 - 39 inches.
COLOR: Body: black with slight bluish-purple gloss; legs, black. Head: black with slight bluish-purple gloss; eyes, brownish gray; bill, black.
FOOD: Omnivorous. See story.
VOICE: Hoarse *kaah, khaan,* or *khaaw;* more melodious than *caw* of American crow.
LIFESPAN: 12 - 17 years.

Did You See Me? Tell Your Story! _____

_____

_____

DID YOU KNOW? I'm close kin to the American crow, just a bit smaller, more slender, and I talk faster. I'm much smaller than cousin Raven, though. His big body and thick bill make him have to hop two or three times when he takes off to fly. Me? I just fly.

Common Raven

dotson' in Koyukon • Corvus corax

I am Raven. You named me "common," but I am common *only* because you see me almost everywhere in Alaska. I live from tundra to forests, rocky coasts to mountains, small villages to cities, migrating only short distances, if at all. Being the largest member of the crow family, I grow to be over two feet long, the largest songbird in the world. I'm larger and heavier than Crow, with a distinct, heavy curve on top of my bill, a long, wedge-shaped tail, and thick, shaggy throat feathers. I make more than thirty *uncommon* croaks, gurgles, whistles, and knocking sounds, plus my deep *kaw* and *crruck*.

During the day, I'm usually with my lifelong partner and a small group. At night, however, hundreds of us may gather to roost. In flight, I am strong and surprisingly acrobatic. A few hops along the ground, then I fly with strong, slow wingbeats, climbing to great heights. I soar like a hawk, my long, flat, wings often sweptback. Alone or with my partner, I twist, turn, roll, somersault, and even hover in one place. I carry sticks and feathers into the air, trade these with my partner, or drop one to chase by myself. Watch as I put on a great show!

I watch you, too, using my keen intelligence to imitate sounds you make, as well as to learn what you do. I know that you discard food. I have meals after your picnics and from your open garbage cans, giant dumpsters, and dumps. Away from town, I pay attention to the loud sound of gunshots. If you hunt, scraps will be left behind. I trick animals into providing food for me, too. I call to wolves, leading them to an animal to kill. They will eat until they are satisfied and leave the rest for me. I dine, then cache the extras, creating clever disguises for my hiding places. My intelligence helps me find clever ways to have you, and others, satisfy my endless hunger and curiosity.

This ability has lead me to being part of the mythology, or old stories, of many cultures. Some stories say I'm a greedy, mysterious creature who tricks others into doing what I want them to do. Several cultures say I have tricks that help people find what they need in life. Others say I change into different forms to get what I want. Some believe I helped create the world and deserve great respect. One famous poet said I was frightening and creepy. Watch me, then tell me what *you* think!

My Facts

SIZE: Length: 22 - 24 inches. Weight: 24 - 40 ounces. Wingspan: 46 - 53 inches.
COLOR: All black with metallic, purplish shine in some lights.
FOOD: Omnivorous. Scavengers, eating wide variety of plants and animals, including grains, small mammals, birds, invertebrates, insects, trash, carrion, roadkill.
VOICE: More than 30 distinct calls, most common are *kaw, kraaak, prruk-prruk-prruk.*
LIFESPAN: 6 - 17 years.

Did You See Me? Tell Your Story! _____

_____

_____

DID YOU KNOW? My mate builds our stick nest high on a cliff or in a tree. The inner cup is made of small twigs and branches lined with mud, fur, and grass. Finished, it is about five feet across and two feet high. Research to find out about our young.

Tree Swallow

tulugagnaurak in Inupiat • Tachycineta bicolor

Oh, hello. I'm Stuart Swallow, a beautiful, acrobatic bird. See how my glossy, blue-green back sparkles in the sunlight? Notice the sharp contrast between my colorful back, dark cap, and snow-white chest and belly? My colors make me stand out from all the other swallows. You must agree that I am very attractive!

Acrobatic? Oh, yes! I do amazing twists and turns, darting one way then another. My long, pointed wings help me zoom after flying insects. My gape, the opening of my mouth, extends very wide to let me take in hundreds of mosquitoes, flies, and other insects. Mornings and evenings, when insects are out, I feed as I roam at least twenty miles, flying low over fields and water. Every day, I eat as many as two thousand insects. I keep *millions* of pesky, flying critters from biting you!

I bathe when I fly, too. I glide and swoop low over water, skimming against the surface, then rise quickly to shake off the extra water droplets. Sometimes I snatch a drink when I skim the surface, gently tapping the water to take a quick sip. I may touch the surface several times in a row, so I look like a pebble skipping across the water. If you want to see something truly amazing, watch for my whole flock to bathe or drink together.

My flock is sometimes hundreds, sometimes hundreds of thousands. We feed, roost, migrate, and winter together. If flying insects swarm, we gather hurriedly to feed on them.

Often, just before sunset, when it's time to sleep, my flock forms a thick cloud above a marsh or grove of trees, swirling like a tornado. Then we make passes over our roosting site. Each time we pass, some of us drop and settle in for the night, all of us eventually bedding down. In late fall, when it's time to migrate, hundreds of thousands of us travel together to Mexico or Central America. Actually, we winter farther north than any other swallows, leaving later in the fall and returning earlier in the spring than they do.

Soon after returning to Alaska, breeding-aged females build grass, feather-lined nests in cavities, or holes in old trees. The best place is in a woodpecker's old home near a marsh, lake, or muskeg. The females lay four to seven white eggs that hatch in less than three weeks. Nestlings fledge in another three weeks. Then all of us are one big flock again! Watch for us to swarm and to swirl. It's an amazing sight!

My Facts

SIZE: Length: 5.5 - 6.25 inches. Weight: 0.5 - 0.7 ounces (about 4 large eggs). Wingspan: 12 - 14.5 inches.
COLOR: Body: upperparts, dark, glossy, metallic greenish-blue (female duller); underparts, snow white; legs, pale brown. Head: nape/crown down over eyes, dark, glossy, metallic greenish-blue; front/throat collar, snow white. Immature: upperparts, brownish; rest like adult.
FOOD: Omnivorous. Summer/fall: insects, including mosquitoes, flies, bees, other flying insects, ants, beetles; also, spiders, mollusks, roundworms. Winter: berries.
VOICE: Song: repeated series of clear, whistled phrases. Call: high, liquid chirping or twittering *weet, ttit, sweet.*
LIFESPAN: 12 years.

Did You See Me? Tell Your Story! _____

_____

_____

DID YOU KNOW? Called a tree swallow because of where our nests are built, I'm a hard worker yet surprisingly tame. I might sit on your shoulder if you are very quiet and still. If you drop a feather, I will chase it just like your puppy chases a ball! Watch!

Black-capped Chickadee

kaatoowu' in Tlingit • Poecile atricapillus

Chip Black-capped Chickadee here, and you will know if I'm around. Why? I tell you who I am when I call out my *chick-a-dee* call. In fact, if you hear me repeat the *dee-dee-dee* sound, you'll know I'm sounding the alarm. Danger is near! Once you hear me, look for a tiny, chubby guy with a large round head, a very short, thick bill, stubby neck, and a long, narrow tail. I'm constantly on the move, hopping and clinging to twigs and branches near the ground. I even hang upside down sometimes! If I fly across a road or open area, I bounce like a ball without hitting the ground. I am very curious about you, so I won't dart away if I see you first.

The truth is I'm a very gentle, sweet, friendly flier who plays extremely well with others. I'm usually with a flock of friends, and I'm not picky about who's in my crowd. Woodpeckers, nuthatches, warblers, and other woodland songbirds join me and my family in either small groups or larger flocks. We are busy when we are all together, too, with activity going on everywhere. Wherever there are trees or woody shrubs, forests, weedy fields, parks, or even your neighborhood, I will be there feeding, foraging, and playing with my friends.

I'll be sure to feed in your neighborhood if you hang out a feeder for me. Put some sunflower seeds, suet, or peanuts in it, and I'll move right in! Don't worry, though.

I'm the neatest eater in the flock. I fly to the feeder and pick out one seed then take it to a tree away from the feeder. There, I peck a hole in the shell, chip out and eat tiny bites of the seed until it's gone. I drop the empty hull where I ate, so there'll be no mess under your feeder. (I always poop away from the feeder, too, and not everyone does that!) I must be honest, though. Sometimes I take seeds to store for later, hiding each one in a different place. Can you believe I never forget where I put them, even when I've stashed thousands of seeds?

These stored seeds help me survive the long Alaska winter. I'm not a traveler, so I'm here all year long. When the temperature drops below zero, I dig myself a cavity, or roosting hole, in a piece of rotten wood. That's where I sleep, cozy and warm! See why I need your feeder?

My Facts

SIZE: Length: 5 - 5.25 inches. Weight: 0.3 - 0.5 ounces (same as the average house key). Wingspan: 6.5 - 8 inches.
COLOR: Body: back, brownish gray; sides, orangish buff; underside, white; wings, dark gray with white edges in center; tail/legs, gray. Head: cap/throat to bill/bill/eyes, black; cheeks/nape, white.
FOOD: Omnivorous. Seeds, berries, other plants, insects, spiders.
VOICE: Song: simple, high whistled *fee-bee-ee;* first note higher in pitch. Call: chattering *chick-a-dee.*
LIFESPAN: 9+ years.

Did You See Me? Tell Your Story! _____

_____

_____

DID YOU KNOW? Our females nest in cavities in dead trees or in nest boxes. They dig out their own holes, use natural ones, or find woodpecker holes. One to thirteen brown-speckled, white eggs hatch within two weeks, and fledging happens by three weeks.

Black-capped Chickadee   43

Red-breasted Nuthatch

ts'ahts'a´a in Haida • Sitta canadensis

Which way's up, or down? Oh, hi. I'm Naomi Nuthatch, creeping up, down, sideways, and all around the trunks and branches of trees in this mature, coniferous forest. I'm looking for food . . a yummy spider, insect, or seed. I use my long, pointed bill to probe for tasty morsels in crevices and under flakes of bark on spruce, fir, and pine trees. With unusually long toes and claws, it's easy for me to run on trees without falling off. I also catch flying insects in the air, making quick, short flights in my bouncy, up-and-down, speedy flight pattern. I even zoom to the feeder in your yard where I wait, taking my turn, to find just the right seed. (I'm picky!) I'm not afraid of you, so if you come close while I'm at your feeder, I may just watch you. If you watch me, you'll see that I'm a tiny, active, intense bundle of energy, moving quickly wherever I am.

I'm especially busy when I work with a mate to build my nest each year. Together, we carve out a hole in an old, decaying tree in a fir or spruce boreal forest. I collect most of the grass, moss, bark fibers, and feathers to form my round, little nest inside this cavity. Then, my mate collects tiny balls of resin, or sticky sap, and smears it all around the outside of the hole. I coat the inside of the opening with the same resin. My mate and I know how to fly straight into the nest without getting stuck in this gooey mess! But the resin stops predators from trying to go inside to our eat our young, and other hole-nesting birds won't try to steal my nest materials. My nest is a safe place for me to lay my four to seven white eggs with pretty reddish-brown spots. These eggs hatch in about twelve days, and my nestlings fledge within three weeks.

When I have my brood of chicks, I'm too busy to hang out with my friends. When I'm not nesting, though, and when I migrate, I join small flocks of chickadees, kinglets, and woodpeckers. Pick me out of the crowd by looking for my reddish breast and the unique markings on my head. I have a blue-gray crown and nape, a thick, white "eyebrow" stripe above each eye, and a black stripe through my eye. Look for my white throat that floats down onto my shoulders. Remember that I may be upside down, too!

My Facts

SIZE: Length: 4.3 - 4.75 inches. Weight: 0.3 - 0.5 ounces. Wingspan: 7.1 - 7.9 inches.
COLOR: Body: upperparts, deep blue-gray; breast/belly, rusty reddish-cinnamon; wings, blue gray with white; legs, brown; female duller. Head: crown/nape, black (male), blue gray (female); eyestripe, inky black; chin/throat/upper eyestripe, white; bill, black. Immature: duller than adult.
FOOD: Omnivorous. Summer/fall: insects, insect eggs, flying insects, spiders, seeds. Winter: seeds, especially those of conifers.
VOICE: Song: rapid, repeated series of *ehn-ehn-ehn.* Call: nasal *yank-yank-yank;* sounds like toy tin horn.
LIFESPAN: 7.5+ years.

Did You See Me? Tell Your Story! _____

_____

_____

DID YOU KNOW? In thick forests, you'll probably hear me before you see me. If you do spot me, I might be storing seeds in crevices in a tree's bark. Using my bill, I hammer the seeds in until the shell breaks, "hatching" the nut. That's how I got my name.

Ruby-crowned Kinglet

ts'ats'e´e in Tlingit • Regulus calendula

Tsee-tsee-tsee, tew-tew-tew, ti-didee, ti-didee, ti-didee! Hear my amazing song? Kingston Kinglet here, singing from the top of this tall spruce tree. I'm sure you'll hear me singing if you're near a coniferous forest, or just about any other wooded area throughout the state. I have one of the biggest, most enthusiastic voices in the forest, and my song lets others know this is *my* territory. I'm tiny, a bit plump, and quite hard to see, especially in the summer when I live way up high in tall conifer trees. I have a voice, though, that makes me sound huge! My long, bubbly, amazingly loud song is like listening to an entire musical aria!

Once you hear me, be alert! I'm a wing flicker, meaning I'm constantly twitching my wings. No one else moves like I do, so that's a sure sign it's me. As I twitch my wings, I frantically forage, or feed. At all levels of trees and shrubs, I find tasty insects or spiders hiding on leaves, twigs, and branches. You might even see me hovering, or flying in the same spot, at the tip of a branch while I'm feasting on a tiny insect. I am a totally nervous, restless, constantly active bundle of energy, darting from here to there, twig to branch, then out into the open air to catch a flying insect. You'll be tired just watching me move!

I dart around alone most of the time, too. I'm rather secretive and more solitary than other songbirds. During migration, I might hook up with a small group of warblers, nuthatches, and chickadees. I like to move south quite early in the fall, however, so I often just take off on my own. I come back later in the spring than others, too, especially my cousin Kingley Golden-crowned Kinglet. We are the only two kinglets in North America, and we're very easy to tell apart. He has a bold, black-and-white facial pattern and gold crown, while my face is not striped. I have a bold, white ring around each eye, and my crown patch is red. You'll have to look closely, though, as those crown feathers are usually hidden. In fact, our females don't have red crowns at all, and I only raise mine when I want to attract a girlfriend, or am very upset by a predator or enemy. That's when you'll see red on me! I'm always flicking wings, though, so watch for twitching!

My Facts

SIZE: Length: 3.75 - 4.5 inches. Weight: 0.2 - 0.3 ounces (weight of one sheet of paper). Wingspan: 6.75 - 7.5 inches.
COLOR: Body: grayish olive; underparts, paler; wings, bright yellow-green with narrow white bar contrasting with blackish bar; legs, dark. Head: eyes, dark with bold white eye-ring; bill, black with lighter edges; crown patch, bright ruby-red (male only).
FOOD: Omnivorous. Spring/summer: insects, including flies, wasps, beetles, bugs, eggs of insects. Fall/winter: plant material, including seeds, berries, oozing sap.
VOICE: Song: See story. Call: husky, dry *ji-dit*.
LIFESPAN: 4+ years.

Did You See Me? Tell Your Story! _____

_____

_____

DID YOU KNOW? Don't be surprised if you see me at your bird feeder, flitting about, flicking my wings. Look for the band on my leg. From 1955 to 2000, hundreds of thousands of us were banded. Please call the phone number on the band if you find me!

Ruby-crowned Kinglet   47

American Robin

dilk'ahoo in Koyukan • *Turdus migratorius*

Oh! *LOOK*! The sun is just coming up! I'm Rosie Robin, most familiar bird in North America, singing from my songpost among these beautiful flowers. Open your sleepy eyes and listen to my rich, clear, caroling song of short phrases that rise and fall in pitch . . . *cheerily-cheer-up, cheerily-cheer-up.* I'm the "harbinger of spring," meaning my song tells people all over the continent that the long winter is over. I don't just sing in the morning, either. Throughout the day, all spring and summer, you'll hear my voice as I move from songpost to songpost, establishing my territory.

In Alaska, that territory will be almost anywhere south of the Brooks Range. Look for me on the tundra, beaches, and muskegs, from high in the mountains to the edges of lowland forests. Watch for me on lawns all over town, including your favorite park. That's where I search for yummy earthworms. I run a few steps, pause, stand tall, then cock my head to look and listen, hoping to locate a juicy worm to tug from the ground.

You already know what I look like! I have a beautiful, red breast on my large, round body, long legs, and a fairly long tail. I'm so well-known that people compare the size of other birds to my size. I've heard people say, "Oh, that sparrow is half the size of a robin," or "Charlie Crow is almost twice as big as Rosie Robin."

People also know me by the color of my eggs . . . robin-egg blue. I find a new mate each spring, and from April to July, I have one to three broods, or hatchings. Each brood has three to five eggs, and each new clutch, or group of eggs, is in a new nest. I build all these nests by myself! Five to twenty-five feet from the ground, usually on the branch of a shrub or tree with thick leaves for camouflage, I form my cup-shaped nests. I press dead grasses, twigs, and feathers together, working mud into them to create a sturdy, heavy nest. I line the cup with fine, dry grass, and other soft materials to make a cushion for my eggs. The eggs hatch in about two weeks, and in another two weeks or so, my hatchlings fledge. It's sad that only about forty percent of my broods produce young, and only twenty-five percent of the fledglings survive to the winter. This doesn't stop my singing, though, so listen for my beautiful song!

My Facts

SIZE: Male slightly larger. Length: 9 - 11 inches. Weight: 2.7 - 3 ounces. Wingspan: 12 - 15 inches.
COLOR: Male: Body: back, dark gray; breast, rusty orange to brick red; throat, white with dark stripes; lower belly/undertail, white. Head: darker than back; bill, yellow; eyes, dark with white crescents above and below. Female: Slightly paler all over. Immature: breast, reddish with large, black spots.
FOOD: Omnivorous. Spring/summer: earthworms, insects, spiders, snails, other invertebrates, berries, fruit. Winter: berries, fruit.
VOICE: Song: See story. Call: varied clucking *pup, piik, tyeep,* or *tut-tut-tut.*
LIFESPAN: 6 - 13+ years.

Did You See Me? Tell Your Story! _____

_____

_____

DID YOU KNOW? Most of us migrate south for the winter, but some stay if the food supply is adequate. Hundreds to thousands of those migrating form communal flocks to roost in trees at night, with smaller flocks foraging for berries during the day.

Varied Thrush

t'a'n in Haida • *Ixoreus naevius*

So, here's the deal. I'm Thomas Varied Thrush, part of the same thrush family as Rosie Robin. In fact, I'm nicknamed the "winter" or "Alaskan" robin by some. My body is similar in size and shape to Rosie's, but my tail is shorter. And I *don't* stand up tall like she does. In fact, I slouch. I'm sure you've heard the chatter about how pretty her red breast is. Well, *I've* heard that *I'm* the most handsome of *all* thrushes in North America. *My* breast is a marvelous orange color, with an amazing, contrasting, black "bib" band that looks incredible with my cool, slate, bluish-gray back and nape. My face is stunning with its orange eyebrow and black eye stripe, and my dark wings have two orange wing bars and some orange edging for contrast. Most handsome? Clearly!

It's clear, too, that I'm not *at all* sweet and cheerful like Rosie. I *don't* hang out with her and her friends, and I *don't* play well with others. I don't even *like* others! I *won't* snack at your bird feeder, as I stay in my space on the ground, foraging *by myself*. If someone tries to join me, I raise my tail to define *my* space. Still there? My head snaps forward as a warning. *Still* there? I attack, poking and pecking, fully intending to do bodily harm. If someone comes into my territory when my mate and I are nesting, that's *BIG* trouble. Singing establishes my territory, and my body lets you know to stay away. I swoop and dive to warn you, but if you come close, I cock my tail, lower my wings, stand to face you, and even spread my tail and wings to let you know I *will* attack! On guard!

Like Rosie, I'm common throughout Alaska, but you probably won't see me. I'm shy and elusive, living mainly in dark, wet, mature, coastal forests. That's where the understory, or lower vegetation, is filled with bushy shrubs, ferns, and other plants. I hide there, foraging on the ground, hopping instead of walking, using my bill to pull leaves out of the way. This exposes the dirt underneath where insects and worms live. I do roam out onto the tundra, tidal flats, and beaches occasionally, but the forest is my safe place. Try to listen for my "song," a single, long, eerie, whistling pitch, a pause, then another whistle at a different pitch. I sound like your grandmother's old phone ringing through the woods. I'm the sound without the source!

My Facts

SIZE: Length: 9 - 10 inches. Weight: 2.5 - 3.5 ounces. Wingspan: 14 - 16 inches.

COLOR: Male: Body: back, slate to dark blue-gray; belly/breast, orange; breast "bib" band, black; wings, dark gray-black with two orange stripes, orange edging on some feathers. Head: slate to dark blue-gray; eyebrow/face, orange. Female: Same pattern with back, paler gray-brown; breast band, gray; muted overall. Immature: like female with whitish belly.

FOOD: Omnivorous. Spring/summer: insects, beetles, spiders, other arthropods, snails, worms, berries. Fall/winter: acorns, nuts, fruit.

VOICE: Song: long, single, eerie, clear or buzzy whistled note on one pitch, long pause, same sound at different pitch. Call: short, low *chup* or *tschook*.

LIFESPAN: 4 - 5+ years.

Did You See Me? Tell Your Story! _____

_____

_____

DID YOU KNOW? How many of us are there? That changes every two to three years depending on the winter's food supply. But our population has been declining because of the cutting down of old-growth trees! *STOP* doing that! You're destroying our homes!

Bohemian Waxwing

diltsooga in Koyukon • *Bombycilla garrulus*

Hey! Wendy Bohemian Waxwing here. I was named "Bohemian" after the free-spirited Bohemian people who wander like nomads. "Waxwing" comes from the red, shiny tips on my secondary feathers that look like the sealing wax people used in the olden days to keep their letters closed. "Wendy?" Well, that's just me.

Do I really roam and wander? I certainly do! Most all migrating birds have a flight plan and return to the same place every winter. Not me. With my flock of hundreds, or even thousands, I go anywhere south, east, or west to find the sweet, sugary berries of mountain ash, juniper, hawthorn, or other trees and plants. I wander through wooded or brushy areas, towns, and other habitats to find my fruit. After eating, my unusually large liver changes the sugar in the fruit to energy that keeps me alive and moving. I have to be careful, though, when I eat older berries that have fermented, meaning the juice has turned to alcohol. If I eat too much fermented fruit, my liver and body can't take care of all the alcohol, and I actually become drunk. That's dangerous, as I might fall out of a tree, or simply die from too much alcohol!

During my winter and spring wanderings, I find my mate for the next breeding season. Males try to attract me by perching near me on a branch, hopping toward me, touching my bill, offering the gift of a tiny bit of food or other object, then hopping away and back several times. If I decide he's the one, I return his gift. Later in the spring, when we all return to the northern boreal forest or the muskeg, my mate and I build our nest in an open area or along the edge of the forest. We don't establish a specific territory to defend, but my mate won't let other males move in on the family. Bill-snapping and threatening posture tell an invader to scram. With no territory to talk about, however, there is no song to sing. Sadly, we are songbirds without a song.

We do *call* sometimes, though, especially to let the flock know where the summer fruit is ripening. Until the fruit is ready, we eat insects, especially flying ones. To catch them, I often fly out from the top of a spruce tree, or circle after them high in the air. This is a good time for you to spot me. I'll be with others, so wave if you see us!

My Facts

SIZE: Male larger. Length: 6 - 8 inches. Weight: 1.5 - 2.5 ounces. Wingspan: 12 - 14.5 inches.
COLOR: Body: grayish brown; wings, small white and yellow patches plus red, wax-like spots at tip of secondary feathers; tail, grayish to black with yellow tip; undertail, chestnut. Head: face, chestnut with white-lined, black mask; crest, grayish brown; eyepatch, black; throat, black patch (male's larger). Immature: lighter gray-brown; throat, whitish; no black under eye; underparts streaked.
FOOD: Omnivorous. Summer: mainly insects, especially flying; berries, fruits as available. Winter: berries, especially mountain ash, juniper; seeds of birch and other trees; oozing sap.
VOICE: Call: harsh, trilling, high-pitched *seeee*.
LIFESPAN: 5+ years.

Did You See Me? Tell Your Story! _____

_____

_____

DID YOU KNOW? Since 1970, Anchorage has been a favorite place for us to live. That's when oil companies built tall buildings here. Landscaping included planting many mountain ash trees. Flocks of us live in town now to feast on the berries in these trees!

Wilson's Warbler

kk'osaaghttugha in Ahtna • Wilsonia pusilla

I'm Walter Wilson's Warbler, named after Alexander Wilson, a famous ornithologist who wrote the first encyclopedia of American birds in the 1800s. Wilson's warblers are one of fifty-two species of wood warblers in North America. Most of us are small, extremely active, brightly-colored insect eaters. I'm mainly bright yellow, with an olive-green back, black cap, and a black, needle-pointed bill for grabbing insects. I'm told *none* of us should be called warblers, though. Our song, a series of short, buzzy, fast notes, sounds like a noisy insect, *not* the melodious, musical song of a warbler. I don't care. . . I know who I am!

I'm an extremely busy little bird, *constantly* on the move. I flit. I fly, low to the ground, hovering, then pecking insects from leaves and twigs. I cock my long tail upward, twitch it in a circle, and flip it from side to side. I flick my wings in and out, up and down, while I hop from branch to branch grabbing a meal. I zoom out to snag insects in midair, too, and might even perch on your finger and look you in the eye. I'm not afraid of you!

If I don't land on your finger or visit your yard, *you* are going to have to look carefully to find me. I hide in brushy, woody thickets near water, especially willow and alder groves near streams and ponds. I don't like thick forests, but I love watery bogs with moist, tangled bushes.

You might even see me at the edge of a beaver pond! Insects are more likely to be in moist places, so that's where I'll be.

Don't look in the winter, for I migrate south in the fall. I'm the *only* warbler who goes to the high plains areas in the far southern tropics of southern Mexico and Central America! We all return in the spring, with the males coming back earlier to claim their breeding territories. They even travel at night to try to get here first! When I arrive, I choose my mate, then find a nest site. This spot will be on the ground under a bush, hidden in a patch of moss or sedge, or in the bottom branches of thick shrubs. Our bulky, open-cup nest holds two to seven creamy-white eggs marked with tiny, reddish spots. In two weeks our chicks hatch, and in another two weeks they begin flying. Within another month, we all flit away, on our own again.

My Facts

SIZE: Length: 4.5 - 5 inches. Weight: 0.5 - 0.8 ounces. Wingspan: 6.5 - 7 inches.
COLOR: Spring/summer: Body: upperparts/wings, darkish olive-yellow; underparts, bright yellow; legs, reddish tan. Head: crown to nape, olive yellow; face, yellowish with orange; caps, male, black, female, dull greenish; eyes, black; bill, brownish. Winter: Both duller. Immature: duller with less cap color.
FOOD: Omnivorous. Mainly insects, including bees, wasps, beetles, aphids; also, some spiders, other small invertebrates, berries.
VOICE: Song: evenly spaced, rapid, staccato series of *chip-chip-chip* with drop in pitch at end. Call: sharp, husky *jimp-jimp* or *timp-timp.*
LIFESPAN: 8+ years.

Did You See Me? Tell Your Story!

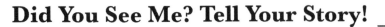

DID YOU KNOW? A subspecies of us here in Alaska is slightly larger but has no orange on its forehead. Its numbers are declining rapidly. Scientists found this group migrates only to one place where resorts have replaced their feeding areas. Tragic!

Yellow Warbler

silaluksiiyaurak in Inupiat • Dendroica petechia

Oh, *NO!* I'm Wanda Warbler, and that lazy Connie Brown-headed Cowbird just dropped one of her eggs in *my* nest! There are very few of her kind in Alaska, but darn, she's here! She never makes her own nest. . . just goes around laying one of *her* eggs in *our* nests. It took me *four days* to build my nest up high in the vertical fork of this willow tree. It's strong, with the cup made of bark, plant fibers, and grasses, lined inside with soft hairs, feathers, and other little fibers. All over the outside I put more strong plant fibers and even spider webs.

I've been incubating *my* five pale-blue, brown-spotted eggs for a week, with only another week until they hatch. My mate and I have protected them from danger, and we're *very* territorial when we are breeding. We did work together with our neighbors, though, to mob and chase away an invading jay the other day. Another day, my mate distracted a red squirrel by flying away from our nest and yelling really loudly at it! Then wouldn't you know it . . . that lazy Connie ruined everything! I *won't* sit on her egg, so now I have to build a new layer of nesting material to cover the thing. The new layer will cover *my* eggs, too, so my brood might not hatch. I might have to lay another clutch. Or maybe not. Oh, it's just *so* upsetting!

I'm *so* pretty I shouldn't have to be upset like this. In North America, there are more than fifty species of warblers, and I'm more uniformly, gorgeously yellow than anyone else. My underparts are bright golden yellow; my back is yellow blended with light olive green; and my face is pure yellow, making my large, black eyes stand out. My wings and tail have yellow edging, and the tiny spots on my short tail are yellow. No one else has spots! (To be honest, though, our males are brighter yellow, and they have reddish streaks on their breasts, which I don't have.)

My coloring makes me easy to see at the tops of willow thickets, or any wet, brushy area, where there are plenty of insects. I'm a restless, busy forager, moving with quick hops along small branches and twigs, snatching a meal with my dark, stout bill. I make short flights, hovering to reach insects on leaves. Given the chance, I'll even forage in your moist greenhouse. Then in a flash, I'll be gone! Pay attention, and look fast!

My Facts

SIZE: Length: 4.5 - 5.5 inches. Weight: 0.3 - 0.8 ounces. Wingspan: 7.8 - 8.0 inches.
COLOR: See story.
FOOD: Omnivorous. Small insects, insect larvae, caterpillars, beetles, some berries.
VOICE: Song: varied bright, musical, whistled *sweet-sweet-sweet; swee-swee-swee-ti-ti-ti-swee.* Call: sharp *chip; hiss* to defend territory; *seet* to defend nest; female single call only.
LIFESPAN: 9 - 11 years.

Did You See Me? Tell Your Story! _____

_____

_____

DID YOU KNOW? We migrate to Mexico or northern South America, and when we return, courtship begins. Males set up territories, then try to attract a female. They sing more than three thousand songs a day and perform fancy flights. It's quite impressive!

Fox Sparrow

chaj xawa'a in Haida • Passerella ilica

Yo! I'm Spaulding Sparrow, a foxy-red fox sparrow. I'm only one of the four color schemes my family wears, ranging from my foxy red to gray to grayish brown to dark brown. Our colors vary more than almost any other bird species! *All* color groups, though, have large, stocky bodies, with rounded heads, and various lengths of stout bills. To make things less confusing for you, I'll just talk about the two groups who summer in Alaska.

So. I'm in the most brightly-marked "red" group, named after the red fox. (Fox sparrow - get it?) Like him, bright rufous (RUE-fuss), or reddish brown, is my dominant color. Streaks of rufous feathers on my back cover the little bits of gray up there, and my white throat and belly are covered with plenty of triangular, rufous spots blending into reddish streaks. The wing bars on my long wings are whitish; my face is gray; and the crown and cheeks of my gray head have rufous patterns. My rump is pure gray, so my relatively short, bright, reddish-brown tail really stands out!

Listen. My song stands out, too, as I wander throughout the taiga (TIE-ja), or spruce and pine forests of Northern Alaska, all the way to Southcentral. (I don't hang out in Southeast or the Aleutians - that's Sooty's territory. I'll tell you about him in a second.) I have the richest, sweetest, most melodious warble of all sparrows. *Too-weet-wiew, too-wert tuck-soo-weet-wiew.* Think you'll recognize me?

Look. To recognize Sooty, look in coastal areas for a small, mostly dark-brown sparrow, with dark-brown tail and wings. He has a whitish belly with lots of large, dark-brown triangular spots. I don't like to gossip, but his song buzzes more than mine and is more choppy. Mine's better.

Ok. *All* of us stay hidden in remote areas, either alone or with a small group of any type of sparrow. I'll be undercover in dense, brushy woods and forests. Sooty goes for willow and blackberry thickets along streams. Everywhere, we make a mess of the leaf-litter on the ground as we look for food. We double-scratch, meaning we hop forward then immediately hop backward dragging both feet through the fallen leaves. This way we uncover insects and seeds. You might hear me scratching around before you see me!

Don't look in the winter, though, as I migrate south to the Lower 48. I'll be hiding there, too, scratching for food.

My Facts

SIZE: Length: 6 - 7.5 inches. Weight: 1.0 - 1.2 ounces. Wingspan: 10 - 11 inches.
COLOR: See story.
FOOD: Omnivorous. Seeds, especially grasses and weeds; insects, including ants, beetles, fly larvae, bees; also, spiders, berries (coastal groups also eat tiny crustaceans and other small marine creatures on beaches).
VOICE: Song and call: varies according to color group.
LIFESPAN: 7 - 10 years.

Did You See Me? Tell Your Story!

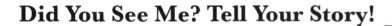

DID YOU KNOW? All color groups live in bushy areas and breed in remote, dense thickets or brushy patches. Three to five heavily-spotted, pale-green eggs are laid in nests built on the ground under shrubs or low in bushes. Guess what color the spots are!

Savannah Sparrow

ts'ats'e´e in Tlingit • Passerculus sandwichensis

Have you seen *me*, Sarah Savannah Sparrow? I'm one of the most numerous, outgoing songbirds in North America, but it's hard to tell me from all the other sparrows. We each have a small, brown body, dark streaks on our backs, and a short, cone-shaped bill for cracking seeds. You'll need to look at my head, breast pattern, and the length and shape of my tail to be sure it's *me*!

I have heavy streaks on my pale breast *and* sides with no central, dark spot. On my small head, I have a pale-yellow or white eyebrow that extends all the way to my bill. A medium-wide, pale stripe runs the length of my crown. Look for my short, notched tail that points downward as I walk, run, or hop on my pink legs. *Now* you'll know it's me!

I'm a grassland sparrow, living in open fields, marshes, weedy areas on the tundra, and subalpine meadows. From the Arctic slope south through all of Alaska . . . that's where I look for food. Spring and summer, I'm close to the ground foraging for seeds, insects, spiders, and bugs. I'm usually with a small flock until the fall. Then my flock begins gathering with other flocks to form a huge group. As winter approaches, the more restless and nervous the big flock becomes. Finally, one dark and stormy night, we all just take off and migrate south to forage in snow-free areas.

In the springtime, when we return to Alaska, many of us go to the same areas where we were hatched. Our males perch on fence posts, low shrubs, and even on the ground to sing their distinctive melodies. At the top of their lungs, each declares its territory and tries to attract a female mate. *If* I become attracted by one of the songs and move toward that male's territory, he flies slowly over the tops of the grass, tail raised, feet hanging down, trying even harder to get my attention.

If his efforts work, we'll raise a family together in a nest I build in one to three days. I hide my nest on the ground in an area of thick, dead grasses surrounded by weeds and sedges. I lay two to six eggs that are different colors. The eggs might be pale, greenish-blue, tan, or white, all with speckles and streaks. My eggs hatch within thirteen days, and in less than a month, my young fly away. Then I'm running around with my friends again, finding seeds and insects! Look for me!

My Facts

SIZE: Length: 4.3 - 6.2 inches. Weight: 0.5 - 1.0 ounces. Wingspan: 7.9 - 9.5 inches.
COLOR: Body: upperparts, gray green with dark streaks; underparts, white with heavy streaks on breast and sides; wings, brown with two pale bands; tail, dark brown; legs/feet, pink. Head: crown, brown with pale stripe down center; eyebrows, pale yellow or white; eyes, brown.
FOOD: Omnivorous. Summer: seeds, insects, spiders. Winter: seeds, berries.
VOICE: Song: descending series of chirps, trills, buzzes *ti-ti, tseeeeee, troooooo.* Call: very high, sharp *stip;* flight call, thin *seep.*
LIFESPAN: 6+ years.

Did You See Me? Tell Your Story! _____

_____

_____

DID YOU KNOW? Famous ornithologist Alexander Wilson named me after seeing me near the city of Savannah, Georgia. He may have "flushed," or frightened me out of hiding in the weeds. That's when I fly up, flare my tail, fly a short distance, and land again.

Dark-eyed Junco

t'adgw in Haida • Junco hyemalis

Jakey Junko here, a "bird of the ground," and one of the most common birds of North America. I live almost everywhere, from sea level to more than eleven thousand feet in the mountains! I'm a unique, lively, medium-sized sparrow with a rounded head, fairly long, notched tail that has beautiful, white feathers on the edges. My bill is short and chunky . . . perfect for cracking seeds. I search for seeds everywhere! I hop near trees and shrubs in open woods and forests, in the undergrowth of brushy, shrubby areas, along roadsides, and in parks and gardens. I *love* looking under your bird feeder since most other birds are terribly messy feeder-eaters. They drop *all kinds* of tasty seeds on the ground. I comb through these, usually finding a feast! Whether I'm foraging alone or with a few others, it might sound like scurrying mice are around. Listen carefully for high *chip-chip* notes. . . that's me searching for food.

If you do hear me, you might be confused about my color. We were once *four* different species, but since 1970, our varied color groups became *one* species with at least six *subspecies*. During Alaska's summer breeding season, *my* slate-colored subspecies is the most widespread and common. Watch for my gray or gray-brown back and head, with my white underside and undertail. You'll find my group almost everywhere south of the Brooks Range. During colder breeding months, I most often look for seeds in Southeast Alaska. That's where the Oregon subspecies hangs out, too.

The birds in that group have a black hood over the head and down the neck, which really stands out against their orangish-brown to light brown back and side feathers. There is some gray in their wings, and the underparts are white. Females of their group have a lighter hood. The truth is, though, *all* our females are less colorful with more dull-brown tones to their feathers.

No matter the color, we are "groupies." Agile flyers, we migrate in large flocks with many other species. We flap our wings continuously and pump our tails to flash our white, outer tail feathers. When we reach the open woodlands and fields of our southern wintering grounds, we form smaller flocks for feeding. You might hear us call *tsick* or *tchet* to keep in touch as our groups spread out.

You might see us *all* suddenly spread out and fly to a tree or bush. One of us just flicked their white tail feathers signaling *Danger!* Did *you* come too close?

My Facts

SIZE: Female smaller. Length: 5 - 6.5 inches. Weight: 0.6 - 1.0 ounces. Wingspan: 7 - 9 inches.
COLOR: All species. Body: solid gray or black; sides, gray, black, or brownish; belly, white; underwings, grayish white; outer tail feathers, white; legs, light. Head: black or gray hood; face, some shade of black or gray; bill, light pink to white; legs, light brown. Immature: same as female except heavily streaked.
FOOD: Omnivorous. Summer: mainly weed and grass seeds; spiders; insects, including beetles, bugs, moths, ants, flies. Winter: seeds, berries.
VOICE: Song: simple, loud, slow, ringing metallic trill on one pitch. Call: very high, hard *stip* or *smack;* in flight, sharp, buzzy *tzeet*.
LIFESPAN: 3 - 11 years.

Did You See Me? Tell Your Story! _____

_____

_____

DID YOU KNOW? Each spring, I attract a mate by singing from the top of a tree. Then I fly to the ground, droop my tail and wings, hop about, and pick up nest twigs. My mate builds our open-cup nest on the ground. She's careful to choose a well-hidden spot.

Dark-eyed Junco   63

Pine Grosbeak

diinyh in Ahtna • Pinicola enucleator

Oh! You are lucky! Momma Greta Grosbeak here, and I'm letting you see into the open cup of my nest. We are about fifteen feet off the ground where a branch meets the trunk of this conifer tree. *I* built this nest of twigs and weeds, then lined it with soft grass. On that grass, I laid three beautiful, blue-green eggs with black, purple, and brown spots. I incubated the eggs for fourteen days, my mate feeding me that whole time. Now, we both feed our young. We carry spiders, insects, and bugs in pouches that grew in the bottom of our mouths before the nestlings were born. In about fifteen days, our young will fledge and be gone. Then my mate and I will go our separate ways to rejoin whatever flocks of finches we choose.

I *am* a finch, the finch of the northern, boreal forest, and the largest of *all* northern finches. My Latin name, *Pinicola*, means "pine dweller," and I absolutely *love* pine trees. The only pines in Alaska are the shore pines of Southeast, so in addition to living there, I'm found in spruce and fir trees in other parts of the state. Check in wet areas along forest edges and openings, and even along dirt roads in the forest! In the spring and summer, look in shade trees, especially fruit trees, in villages and cities. A flock of us will feed in the same tree, enjoying buds and finding seeds in the fruit. We'll stay in that tree until the food is gone, we are full, or something frightens us away. During the winter, I may be in town, but I'll probably be foraging in mixed coniferous and deciduous forests. Watch for me on the ground, in shrubs, as well as in trees.

I'm looking for seeds, since those make up the majority of my diet. To crack them open, I have a thick, stubby, cone-shaped bill. It's so strong I easily crack yummy, black-oil sunflower seeds! If you put *those* seeds in your feeder, look for a bird about the size of a robin who's a bit more plump and heavy chested. You'll see that my tail is long and slightly notched. Look on nearby tree branches, too, where sometimes I sit completely still. You might walk quite close to me without even knowing I'm there. And, if you hoot the single, short whistle of a Pygmy owl, then repeat it, you *might* convince me to come even closer to you! Can you whistle like that owl?

My Facts

SIZE: Length: 8 - 10 inches. Weight: 1.8 - 2.1 ounces. Wingspan: 13.5 - 15 inches.
COLOR: Body: See "Did You Know?"; wings, black to blackish brown with two pale bars; undertail coverts, whitish and gray; legs/tail, black. Head: bill, black; eyes, cinnamon to dark brown.
FOOD: Omnivorous. Mountain ash and other berries, black-oil sunflower and other seeds, fruit, buds; some insects, spiders, bugs; special treats, apple slices, suet, millet, peanuts.
VOICE: Song: rich, clear, caroling warble with trills and softly whistled notes; series of musical warbles. Call: three to four note *teu-teu-teu* or *pe-pew-pew* with middle notes higher.
LIFESPAN: 9+ years.

Did You See Me? Tell Your Story! _____

_____

_____

_____

DID YOU KNOW? Our males are gray, with rosy red on their heads, backs, and underparts. My gray body, with yellow on my head and back, is not quite as striking. Our young look like me the first year, then red begins appearing on the males, too.

Common Redpoll

dildagga in Koyukan • Acanthis flammea

Hey! I'm anything *but* common! Reggie Redpoll's the name, and I should be called Super-bird! I'm a small, winter finch of the arctic tundra and boreal forest, living on land all around the Arctic Ocean. It's incredibly cold this far north, but my super-body survives temperatures as low as sixty-five degrees below zero. My plumage is thirty percent thicker in the freezing wintertime, and I fluff up fully to stay warm. Also, I have two pouches in my throat that hold seeds. I gather seeds on open ground or in low shrubs in weedy fields, brushy tundra, and open thickets. It's much colder in those open areas, plus my enemies can see me more easily. So I gather seeds quickly, store them in my pouches, then zoom back into the protection of birch, willow, or alder trees. There, I take my time to finish eating and digesting my food.

I don't gather seeds nor eat alone. I'm *social*, always with a flock, except when I'm with my breeding mate. (Even then you might find me with a small crowd.) I'm *lively*, constantly moving, restless, busy . . . fluttering and climbing in bushes and open woods. I even hang upside down trying to pry seeds loose from catkins, those long, seedy spikes on some bushes and trees. Sometimes a huge flock of us forages for seeds on the ground then, *whoosh*! We become a chattering mass, swirling away to perch in trees. Even at night there is always *someone* in the flock twittering or fidgeting. It's annoying!

The truth is, I don't like everyone all the time, and I argue. I fluff out my feathers, stand face-to-face with him (or her), open my bill, and jut out my chin. This lets them know I'm not happy with what's going on. In five seconds, though, I'm over it and will share a seed with this same character. You may even see me pass seeds at your backyard feeder in the wintertime, a favorite spot where most of us are very tame and polite.

At your feeder, you'll probably hear my chitter chatter before you see me. Look for the red "poll," or cap, on my forehead, the stubby, yellow bill on my dark face, and my black chin. My sides and rump have dark streaks that stand out against my lighter underfeathers. The seeds in your feeder won't be enough for us, though, if there's a low seed crop on the trees. So wave goodbye . . . we'll be headed south to find food!

My Facts

SIZE: Length: 4.7 - 5.5 inches. Weight: 0.4 - 0.7 ounces. Wingspan: 7.5 - 9 inches.
COLOR: Body: light gray-white with dark streaks (more streaks on sides like vest); breast, female, white, male, deep rosy-pink; wings, dark with two narrow, white bands; legs/feet/tail, black. Head: forehead/cap, red; face around bill/chin/throat, black; bill, yellow. Immature: same except no red cap until end of first summer.
FOOD: Omnivorous. Summer: seeds, including those of small conifers, birch catkins, weeds, grasses; buds of alder, willow, birch; wildflowers; berries; some spiders, insects. Winter: seeds, mainly birch and alder; from feeders, thistle, nyjer (thistle), black-oil sunflower, millet.
VOICE: Song: combined trills or repeated calls *chit-chit-chit-chit*. Call: when perched, buzzy *swe-ee-et* that rises in pitch.
LIFESPAN: 8+ years.

Did You See Me? Tell Your Story! _____

_____

_____

DID YOU KNOW? We live and breed all over the world, staying in the snow and cold as long as there is food. To stay warm in extreme cold, I roost in a snow tunnel four inches deep and a foot long. The snow insulates me against the frigid air. Strange, but true!

Pine Siskin

ts'ahts'a´a in Haida • *Carduelis pinus*

Yipeee! You have small, *nyjer* (NY-ger) seeds in your feeder! My favorite! I'm Sylvie Siskin, here with a few of my flock thoroughly enjoying our meal. Watch me climb, hang upside down, and twitter constantly while I feast on these tasty seeds. When I don't find a backyard feeder, I forage in meadows, weedy fields, scrubby thickets, or other grassy places where seeds grow.

My *favorite* places to eat, though, are conifer forests or mixed woods with conifer and deciduous trees. That's where I flit and dart through the treetops, clinging to branch tips. Sometimes I even hang upside down, pulling seeds out of the bottoms of cones. (My unique, sharply pointed bill is perfect for this!) I'm known as the tiny finch of the evergreen forests, and you might hear me make one of my soft calls. You're more likely to hear our males, though. They love to *trilllll* from treetops then make a wheezy *chirp.* That's why we're nicknamed "pine chirper." Sometimes the males even sound like a chainsaw with their loud *ZZZzzzzzzzzre!*

Once you hear their voices, look for me. My tiny, brown body has dark streaks all over. I'm hard to see in the trees, so watch for tiny yellow flashes. The flight feathers on my pointed wings have yellow streaks, and there are yellow markings on my deeply-notched tail. The amount of this bright color varies on each of us, but we are *all* streaked! (See me hiding behind the feeder in the drawing? Can you fill in my missing streaks?)

Did You See Me? Tell Your Story! _____

_____

_____

There won't be just me, either. I'm always with a tight flock, moving from habitat to habitat. Our large winter flocks are nomadic, meaning we wander from one end of the continent to the other, always searching for seeds. It's difficult to find food in the winter, so when we do find a good supply, we often forget that we are friends. Even *I* become aggressive and competitive toward flock-mates at times. I'll lower my head, spread my wings and tail, then make quiet, threatening calls. I might even lunge at my flock-mate, which usually leads to a fight!

I don't fight that much, though, and I find my next breeding mate in the large, winter flock. When spring comes and we are all back in the open, coniferous forest, my mate and I build our nest. We find a well-hidden spot on a horizontal branch that's away from the trunk. We usually build our nest near others' nests, and we visit each other as we raise our chicks! You can visit, too!

My Facts

SIZE: Length: 3 - 5 inches. Weight: 0.5 - 0.55 ounces. Wingspan: 8.5 - 9 inches.
COLOR: Body: upper, brown with heavy, dark streaking; underparts, lighter with heavy, dark streaking; wings, dark with light edging; tail, brown with yellow edging; legs, dark brown. Head: light with heavy streaking; throat, white with brown streaking; eyes/bill, brown.
FOOD: Omnivorous. Summer: seeds of pines, conifer and deciduous trees, grasses, weeds, flowers; buds of willows, elms; stems of weeds, flowers; some insects, spiders. Winter: seeds.
VOICE: See story; also varied long, buzzy, husky sounds, rising *tee-ee.*
LIFESPAN: 8+ years.

DID YOU KNOW? Our numbers are declining! One reason is salmonella, a bacteria that spreads at backyard feeders that are not cleaned properly. If large flocks of us, or other birds, visit your feeder, please clean it often. That will help us stay healthy!

Common Bird Group Names

Bird	Group Name	Bird	Group Name
grouse, ptarmigan	pack, covey	swallows	flight
harriers	cast, kettle, harassment	chickadees	banditry
eagles	convocation	nuthatches	jar
cranes	sedge, herd	kinglets	castle, court, dynasty
owls	parliament	robins	round
hummingbirds	charm, bouquet	thrushes	hermitage, mutation
belted kingfishers	crown, rattle	waxwings	ear-full, museum
woodpeckers	descent	warblers	confusion, stream, sweetness
falcons	cast	fox sparrows/sparrows	slyness/host, den
jays	party, scold, band	juncos	crew, flutter, host
magpies	murder, charm, tiding	grosbeaks	gross
crows	murder, muster, hoard	redpolls	gallup
ravens	unkindness, congress	siskins	charm, company

Beaks are Bills!

GusGus Spruce Grouse here to tell you that bills and beaks are the same thing . . . it's just a different word for the same part on our bodies. Bills are made out of keratin, the same material as your fingernails. The most important ways we use our bills are to catch and eat food and to feed our young. In addition, we move and hold objects with our bills as well as clean our feathers. Some birds use their bills to fight with other birds and even kill their prey.

What we eat determines the type and shape of our bill. Knowing what these look like will help you identify us. Here are some common bill shapes, uses, and examples of birds who have this bill.

① thin, pointed tweezer-like for catching insects/prey (some warblers, kingfishers)

② large, curved, razor-sharp tip for tearing prey/meat (falcons, hawks, eagles)

③ short, slender for eating small seeds, fruits, plants (some chickadees, swallows)

④ sharp, pointed for eating varied plants/animals (crows, ravens)

⑤ short, thick, cone-shaped for cracking seeds (some finches, sparrows)

⑥ long, pointed, flat on end for boring into bark (woodpeckers)

⑦ long, slim, rounded end for probing into flowers (hummingbirds)

⑧ hooked, sharp tip for shredding meat (owls)

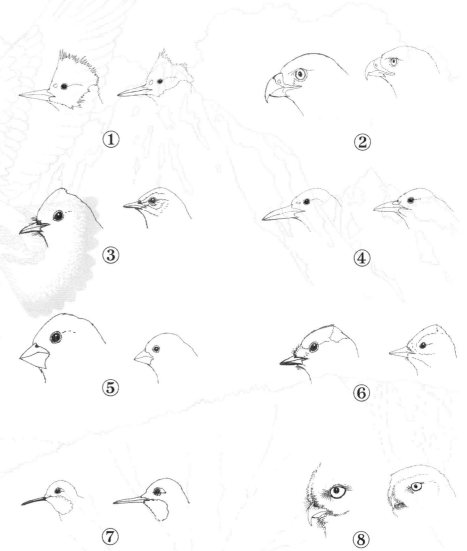

Glossary

amphibian *(am-FIB-e-an)*: cold-blooded vertebrate (animal with a backbone) that lives partly in water and partly on land, found mostly in Southeast Alaska: salamander, newt, frog, toad

barring *(BAR-ing)*: straight stripes, bands, or lines of feathers that are longer than they are wide

biome *(BY-ome)*: area of land with specific climate, plants, and animals, including tundra, deciduous and coniferous forests, deserts, and grasslands

boreal *(BOR-e-al)*: cold, wet area in the far north
boreal forest: has conifer trees (see taiga)

bract *(brakt)*: special, small leaf in the cones of trees that holds seeds

cache *(kash)*: store food to eat later

carrion *(CARe-re-en)*: the carcass and remains of any dead animal

carnivore *(CAR-ni-vore)*: an animal who eats only meat
a **carnivorous** *(car-NIV-or-ous)* animal

catkin *(CAT-kin)*: long, hanging group of flowers with bracts but no petals, found in willows, birches, oaks, and other trees

cavity *(CAV-i-tea)*: a small hole inside a tree trunk, branch, or other surface

clutch: the eggs laid at one time

conifers *(KOH-nuh-fer)*: trees and bushes that are green all year, have needle-shaped or flat, scaly leaves, and grow cones (pine, spruce, fir)
a **coniferous** *(con-NIF-er-ous)* tree

deciduous trees *(de-SIJ-u-ous)*: trees that shed their leaves every year

estuary *(ES-tchew-ary)*: where the fresh water of a river connects with the saltwater ocean, often called the "mouth of a river"

fledge: when nestlings fly away from the nest
fledgling: the young bird who flies away from the nest

forage: to search for food

habitat: the area where an animal lives and grows: tundra, mountains, shoreline, grasslands, etc.

herbivore *(ERB-a-vore)*: an animal who eats only plants
an **herbivorous** *(er-BIV-er-ous)* animal

incubate *(IN-cue-bate)*: to sit on eggs keeping them warm until they hatch

bract

catkin

estuary

insectivore *(in-SECT-a-vore)*: an animal who eats only insects
an **insectivorous** (in-sec-TIV-er-ous) animal

invertebrates *(in-VER-ta-brate)*: cold-blooded animals with no backbone: insects, spiders, crustaceans, worms, etc.

iridescent *(ear-a-DESS-ent)*: shiny or shimmery color that looks like different colors from different angles

morph *(morf)*: a gradual, complete change in plumage from one color to another

muskeg *(MUSK-egg)*: a swampy area with thick, decaying plants often covered with moss

nest box: a birdhouse

nyjer seeds *(NY-ger)*: seeds from the African yellow daisy, also called thistle seeds

nyjer seeds

omnivore *(OM-ni-vore)*: an animal who eats both plants and animals
an **omnivorous** *(om-NIV-or-ous)* animal

ornithologist *(or-ni-THOL-o-gist)*: a person who studies birds

plumage *(PLU-midge)*: the color, pattern, and arrangement of feathers that cover a bird

resin *(RES-in)*: sticky, gooey substance in the outer cells of trees, usually yellow or brown

roost (n): the perch, cage, house or place where birds sleep or rest
 (v): to sit or rest on a perch

sedges: grass-like plants or bushes

stoop: when birds fly or dive down swiftly in order to attack prey

subalpine: a region on mountain slopes where trees grow that is just below timberline

swoop: to fly quickly to a lower elevation

taiga *(TIE-gah)*: biome with coniferous forests, usually pine, spruce, and larch, that's sometimes called boreal or snow forest; world's largest land biome

thickets: where bushes or trees grow closely together

tundra: inland, flat, treeless arctic region where ground is usually frozen below the surface

sedges

Learn More About Land Birds of Alaska

Websites for bird viewing in Alaska

http://www.adfg.alaska.gov/index.cfm?adfg=viewing.main

http://www.adfg.alaska.gov/index.cfm?adfg=birdviewing.hotspots

http://www.alaska.org/things-to-do/birding

http://www.alaska.org/destination/kenai-peninsula/birding

http://www.anchorage.net/discover/wildlife/birdwatching/

http://ak.audubon.org/birding-alaska

Websites to learn more about birds

http://kids.nationalgeographic.com/animals/hubs/birds/

http://www.sciencekids.co.nz/sciencefacts/animals/bird.html

http://kids.sandiegozoo.org/animals/birds

http://www.ducksters.com/animals/birds.php

http://www.kidzone.ws/animals/birds1.htm

Books

National Geographic Kids Bird Guide of North America

Birds, Nests & Eggs (Take Along Guides)

Backyard Birds (Field Guides for Young Naturalists)

Guide to the Birds of Alaska   Robert Armstrong

National Audubon Society: Field Guide to Birds

Peterson First Guides: Birds

The Sibley Field Guide to Birds of Western North America